Birthdays
- A Celebration -

Marilyn Atyeo • Anna Uhde

Illustrations by Jean Allen

Humanics Limited * Atlanta, Georgia

HUMANICS LIMITED
P.O. Box 7447
Atlanta, Georgia 30309

Copyright © 1984 by Humanics Limited. All rights reserved. No part of this book may be reproduced by any means, nor transmitted, nor translated into a machine language, without written permission from Humanics Limited.

PRINTED IN THE UNITED STATES OF AMERICA

Second printing 1987

Typography by Daniel R. Bogdan

Library of Congress Cataloging in Publication Data

Atyeo, Marilyn, 1932-
  Birthdays: a celebration.

  1. Children's Parties.   2. Birthdays.   I. Uhde, Anna, 1947-   . II. Title.
  GV1205.A89 1984   793.2'1   83-83303
  ISBN 0-89334-075-8

Contents

Introduction 5

PLANNING THE PARTY 6
    Making Choices 6
    Choosing a Theme 6
    Selecting the Site 6
    Selecting the Time of Day 7
    Deciding Whom to Invite 7
    Special Family Plans in Addition to or Instead of a Party ... 8

PREPARATION FOR A PARTY 8
    Using Illustrations 8
    Invitations 9
    Decorations 9

DEVELOPMENT OF SOCIAL SKILLS 10
    Discussions 10
    Role Play 10
    Modeling 10
    Coaching 11
    At the Party 11

PARTY COUNTDOWN 11
    Time 11

THE PARTY 12

AFTER THE PARTY 13

1

Birthdays with Friends

    Clown Birthday Party 16
    Mouse Birthday Party 19
    Puppet Birthday Party 23
    Teddy Bear Picnic 26
    Come as a Bum Birthday Party 30
    Cinderella's Dress Up Birthday Party 33

2

Birthday Cooks

    A Birthday Stew 38
    Do It Yourself Birthday Party 43

3

Birthdays Here and There

Space Wars Birthday 48
Community Helpers Birthday Rally 52
CB Truckers Birthday Rally 55
Old McDonald's Barnyard Birthday Fling 58
Pirate Birthday Bash 61
Birthday Record Hop 65

4

Birthdays Around the World

Leprechaun Hideaway Birthday 70
Jolly Old England Birthday Celebration 73
Animal Safari Birthday Party 77
Pizza Birthday Festival 83
Birthday Roundup 86
Japanese Birthday Tea Party 91
Mexican Patio Party 96
Chinese Dragon Party 101
Hawaiian Luau Birthday 105

5

Birthdays Around the Calendar

Snowman's Birthday Party 110
Historical Heroes Birthday Celebration 113
Hearts and Flowers Birthday Party 116
Kite Party 120
April Fool's Backwards Birthday Party 123
Spring Birthday Fest 127
Goin' Fishin' 131
Water Carnival Birthday 135
School Daze Birthday 139
Halloween Happening 143
Harvest Birthday Gathering 147
Toyland Birthday Party 151

Appendix 155

Introduction

What can be more wonderful in the life of a child than his birthday? That special day on the calendar is a landmark that indicates he is a little older, a little bigger, and able to conquer new challenges.

Parents, aware of the importance of this date, seek ways to provide a celebration fitting for the occasion. Unfortunately, they are often apprehensive and unsure about how to plan, prepare, and oversee parties that will be appropriate for the age level and current interests of the birthday child and his friends.

This birthday book was written with the total family in mind. Party suggestions are designed to assist a family in organizing and planning activities that provide excitement and joy for all who share in the festivities. Mom and dad, rather than feeling frustrated as they stage an elaborate fiasco, will cherish enjoyable and close moments with their children as they plan and prepare as well as give the party together. The birthday child will have that "grown-up" feeling as he orchestrates party plans. Brothers and sisters, involved in party preparation and fun, will feel fewer pangs of jealousy. And, the focus on guests will be on seeing that they have a wonderful time, rather than regarding them merely as bearers of gifts.

Parties can be excellent teaching opportunities. Through planning and participating in a party, children can grow intellectually and socially. When the family discusses the alternatives together and makes group decisions about party plans and preparations, children develop objective thinking and problem-solving skills. The spirit of cooperation is enhanced as the family team works together. Explaining the basic four food groups and allowing the child to help in choosing menu items fosters an appreciation and understanding of good nutrition. Games and activities promote social, emotional, and physical development as well as challenge mental skills.

As professionals in early childhood education attuned to the developmental levels of young children, we sought to closely correlate games and activities to skills and interests typical of ages and stages of children. In party themes with multi-level appeal, a variety of alternative activities are available, so it will be easy to select ones most appropriate for the birthday child and his friends. The games and activities are easy, adaptable, and flexible. If the ones included under a theme grouping do not particularly appeal, look through the book and adapt some other games.

The book is primarily offered as a birthday party planning guide for parents, but it has many other uses. Families may want to have a party to celebrate an event other than a birthday. Teachers in day care, kindergarten, and primary schools can glean hints for organizing classroom special events. It may prove most valuable as a resource for activities for rainy days or other times when a child pleads, "What shall we do now, Mommy?"

Planning the Party

Making Choices

A birthday party should be a family affair that encourages all members to share ideas and contribute to preparations. Surprise parties, which tend to promote secretive behavior and cause suspense and trauma, are discouraged. Instead, we recommend that the birthday child, with guidance from parents, have a major responsibility in deciding what will happen on his special day. The following suggestions will help in making party plans and preparations. There is also a timetable and checklist available to help parents to organize, plan, prepare, and give a party.

Choosing a Theme

Well in advance of the special day (about two weeks) decide if there is to be a party, where it will be held, and what the theme will be. The birthday child and his parents will enjoy browsing through this book together. Discuss the party themes and ideas, and then decide which might best fit family needs. If the child is particularly fascinated with a theme such as "Snowman's Birthday Party," but his birthday is in June, consider how, with a few changes, it could be made appropriate. While a little more difficult, it can also be fun to adapt ideas from several themes to create your own special party!

Discuss the menus. Do the foods appeal? Change any food suggestions that the birthday child does not like. Check to make sure the materials needed for decorations are available. If not, decide on substitutions. Consider possibilities for favors and prizes. These need not be elaborate but should be appropriate. (What little boy wants to get a hair bow?) Look at the games and activities suggested. Which ones are suitable for the space available, the number of children to be invited, and their interests? As the birthday child and family discuss the party suggestions and think of alternatives, jot them down so ideas will not be forgotten.

Selecting the Site

The parties we have included are all fun-filled and active. As you select the area in your home where children will congregate, keep in mind that they are not to be expected to sit around like Victorian ladies and gentlemen!

Weather permitting, the ideal places around the home to have a party are the garage, patio, or backyard. There is plenty of space to move freely and no need to worry about spills! If the outside area is to be used, arrange to have all party items readily available. This will save you steps and better insure constant adult supervision.

If it is not possible to have the party in the above areas, the family room or play room will probably be well suited for active games. (Most of these recreational rooms have soil-resistant furniture and spillproof floors.) Many are equipped with snack bars so that food can be served in the room. Even rooms designed for activity need careful scrutiny. Be sure all breakable objects are removed. Toys and playthings can be distracting to children so it is better to put those that are not needed for the party out of sight.

If you must have the party in the living room, be sure to remove all valuable or breakable accessories to another area. Accidents can and do happen! To minimize the use of furniture, push pieces against the walls and rearrange to make an open area where children can participate in games. If possible, serve refreshments in the kitchen or dining area rather than in the living room.

Several birthday themes take children into the kitchen area where they mix, pour, and stir the birthday treats. Scan the work area with a careful eye. Remove any dangerous or breakable items and arrange for ample work space. Supply a sufficient number of plastic bowls and unbreakable utensils so each child "can get his hands into the pie."

A few parties take children to parks, playgrounds, and natural settings, such as a nature trail or fishing pond. When responsible for young children, be familiar with the site and confident that it is safe. Visit the area ahead of time. Carefully check for safety hazards or problem areas. Even though you may feel silly, get down on your knees and look around to gain a child's-eye view of the area. Problems that would have been missed otherwise may become obvious! If the party is planned in an open nonconfined area, be sure to have other adults along who will help assume responsibility for supervision.

Selecting the Time of Day

The hours for the party are critical for younger children. Ideally, the best time is mid-morning. Stay away from early afternoon hours since this is usually nap time. Many children need a nap before regaining good spirits, so a party at this time could be disastrous.

If both parents work, they may find that early evening may be the most convenient time for them, and even the younger children who have had a good afternoon nap will be ready for fun. The length of the party is also very important. For tots an hour to an hour and a half is ample time to be involved in a group activity.

During the school year, school-aged children will need to schedule parties in the later afternoon, early evening or on weekends. Parties that encourage active group participation need not be long. Two to two and a half hours is sufficient time to carry out activities.

Many party themes listed in this book emphasize nutritious meals. The best time to schedule these parties is during lunch and dinner hours. Be sure to inform the parents of the guests that the party includes a full meal.

A party should end promptly with all guests leaving about the same time. You can control this by making arrangements for the host to deliver children back home after the party.

Deciding Whom to Invite

Ask the birthday child to suggest names of those he would like to invite to the party. Since the number attending must be reasonable, some difficult decisions may need to be made. When considering a party for preschool children, a practical suggestion is to invite only one or two more guests than the birthday age of the child. This means that a birthday party for a three-year-old would be limited to four or five children. Older children will want to invite a larger group. Just be sure to limit the size of the party to a manageable number of guests.

Parents of very young children (one to three) will plan to accompany their children at the party. Since this birthday is as much for the family's pleasure as the child's, grandparents, aunts, uncles, and other relatives might like to be honored guests. These parties will need to include two menus, one for tots and one for adults. Older children (four and up) might prefer to not invite relatives to their birthday celebration, but to share a piece of cake and open presents from family at another time.

Do not be surprised to find your child has biased ideas about who to invite. Preschool children will probably mention the names of boys and girls who are regular playmates in the neighborhood or day care center. Children between seven and ten are likely to specify that only guests of their sex be invited. Older children may wish to invite both boys and girls. If a mixed party is planned, be sure to keep the party moving at a fast pace with active participation for all. This is important because of the tendency of children in pre-adolescence to shyly gravitate to boy and girl corners.

Guests should be acquainted and be good friends of the birthday child. It is not wise to invite a child simply because the parent happens to be a friend of yours! Children take time to get acquainted, so a two-hour session among strangers could be very uncomfortable for a newcomer to the group.

Since the number of guests invited to parties for young children is so limited, it is important that all who are invited can attend. Ask each guest to R.S.V.P. or check possible conflicts with parents before sending out invitations.

For both younger and older children we recommend that at least two adults be present to help at the party. If both parents cannot be present, ask a good friend or teenager to help. Unless they have been specifically asked to help, consider relatives and parents who are accompanying their own children as guests.

Special Family Plans in Addition to or Instead of a Party

In addition to the actual party there are many other ways this landmark day can be observed. The child can plan the birthday dinner so that the menu includes his or her favorites. The family may also participate in a special activity selected by the birthday child. This might be a visit to grandparents, a picnic in the park, or a trip to the zoo.

Let the child alter something in the daily routine. The older child might plea, "Please let me stay up as late as I like!" or "Since it is my birthday, can someone else empty the dishwasher?" The younger child is likely to request the reverse. He can be expected to waken at the crack of day or suggest he is now big enough to assume some responsibility or privilege. For example, the mother of three-year-old Meredith was amused when, on her birthday, her daughter stated, "Now that I am a big girl, I can open the door for you and daddy!"

You might think of holding the party at the school, but we do not recommend this idea. It is difficult for the teacher and often against school rules. It is usually permissible and enjoyable, however, to share a birthday treat such as ice cream and cookies with all classmates. School schedules are often rather inflexible so carefully arrange with the teacher the best time of the day to serve treats. She will probably suggest after lunch or during recess.

Preparation for a Party

Preparation can be as much fun as the actual party. To prevent last-minute frenzy, collect materials for invitations, decorations, and favors and begin making items well in advance.

Using Illustrations

Each party theme is introduced with an illustration. This picture can be used in many ways. It can be used to decorate the invitation, the table centerpiece or the cake. It can be used in games and as a springboard for other creative activities.

If a theme picture is used as the invitation figure it will need to be reduced in size. Cut a double form out of construction paper leaving the left side or top attached (the technique is similar to making paper doll chains). Decorate the outside cover and write the message on the inside. Another method is to fold a piece of construction paper in half and then paste the cut-out figure on the cover.

To make a centerpiece for the table, cut a double form out of posterboard or heavy cardboard. Attach at the top, then spread at the base. To keep upright shape, fasten with pins, tape or wire around a basket, a piece of oasis, Styrofoam, or a block of wood.

Games, often a variation of "Pin the Tail on the Donkey," will need to have the figure enlarged. Use the appropriate page in this book with an opaque projector or make a transparency for an overhead projector to enlarge the figure to almost any size. If projecting equipment is not available, copy the figure on graph paper, then enlarge two or three times.

Refer to the Appendix for special instructions on using patterns in this book to decorate the birthday cake with icing and cake-decorating equipment. Figures can also adorn the cake by standing upright. Cut a double form out of construction paper and decorate. Insert a popsicle stick or a few toothpicks between figures before pasting. Be sure sticks extend at least an inch out of the bottom of double form. When glue is dry, insert sticks into the cake.

Most party ideas have additional illustrations included. Some can be enlarged as suggested. Most are included as visual clues so that directions can be clearly understood.

The illustrations for parties are provided as an inspiration for the party theme and can be a real aid to those who find freehand drawing difficult. Don't feel confined to using only our suggestions, though. In particular, minimize the use of patterns by children. If the outline pattern is used by children, encourage them to be creative as they color and add features.

Invitations

Make the invitations first. All children, even the smallest, can have a hand in helping to make colorful invitations. The younger child can draw a picture, help with pasting, dictate the message, and address envelopes.

Do not pass out party invitations to selected friends at school or other places where an uninvited child could have hurt feelings. To be excluded from something that peers will be doing is a terrible experience! We suggest that invitations be hand delivered or mailed to the home address. Ask on each invitation for an R.S.V.P. since the number of guests coming to the party is important to its success.

Decorations

After invitations are sent, the party child, with assistance from family members, can create placemats, name cards, wrapping paper for favors, and decorations. Make a list of needed items for construction. Take a trip to the store for supplies not available around the house.

Having to clean up after only a short work period can be very discouraging, and materials scattered all over the house can be distressing even to parents who are not picky housekeepers. Circumvent these problems by defining a specific work center for constructing party items. The center can be a card table or desk. Supplies and construction materials should be stored nearby in a box or caddy. During party preparation keep the center readily available. The child needs to have the option of enjoying work for brief periods and then changing activity when tired. Supplies should include: magic markers, crayons, scissors, pencils, erasers, glue, colored construction paper, transparent tape and masking tape, and a collection of scrap materials such as yarn, buttons, rickrack, felt, and fabric.

Good organization and housekeeping also includes finding storage space for completed party items. Clear a shelf or drawer and designate it for this purpose. If shelving is scarce, place completed items in a large box that can be stored under the table or desk.

When the child is working on creations, take the time to lend a helping hand, but *don't* impose your ideas. Too much direction is discouraging and makes the child less confident in his ability to do a good job. Enjoy a few moments helping to color, cut, and paste. During these relaxing "together times" a lot of serious discussions can occur. These will likely become some of those moments to always be cherished.

Development of Social Skills

The foundation for social behaviors such as good manners, graciousness, and other accepted cultural skills is established while a child is quite young. These behaviors are not innate in the individual but are acquired as learned behaviors. Even though the young child is egocentric and often not mature enough to fully understand feelings of others, his keen mind picks up clues of appropriate responses. Through observing parents, important adults, and older children, he is alerted to expected social graces. When phrases like "please," "thank you," and "you're welcome" are used at home, it is typical for a child to mimic their use. In the desire to please important adults in his life he will also accept coaching and recommendations as to what should be done.

If social responses are to be internalized and become habit, children need many opportunities to practice what they see and hear. A birthday party can provide an important real moment when skills can be put to practical use. The following ideas are examples of practicing social skills prior to the party.

Discussion

Ask the birthday child how he would feel if he heard others talking about a party and he was not invited. Guide him to the realization that invitations are sent to the child's home and party plans are not discussed at school because of consideration for those not invited.

Role Play

The first few minutes of a party are devoted to welcoming guests and helping them feel comfortable. Practice greetings by having a sibling or playmate pretend to be a guest ringing the doorbell. The birthday child opens the door and says something like, "Bob, I am glad you came to my party." He can then pretend to show the guest where to place his wraps and presents.

Modeling

Introductions need not be formal, but are very important when children meet. Parents can provide a model by showing how guests are introduced to each other. Siblings or playmates can pretend to be guests. Say, "Susan this is Jill." Also, add a conversation starter like, "Jill, what did you and your daddy see at the zoo last week?" Before the party have "play like sessions" in which the birthday child introduces the dog to cat, mom to dad, or dolls to each other.

Coaching

Ask the birthday child what he should say when receiving a gift. In addition to "thank you," suggest he add comments about each gift, such as, "This model car is neat."

Children are embarrassed over the unexpected. Help your child anticipate that some presents may be duplicates of something he already has or might even be a game he does not like. Suggest he say a simple "thank you." Do not encourage fibs but help him appreciate the importance of not saying anything that might make the guest feel uncomfortable.

Parents of guests can also coach social responses. Ask, "What do you say when Sally thanks you for the gift?" The parent of the guest should remind the child to say to both birthday child and his parents, "I had a good time at your party. Thank you for inviting me."

At the Party

Despite the coaching, remember that children have not perfected use of phrases such as "please," "thank you," "you are welcome." In the excitement of the moment they may seem to have forgotten everything! If you can give a whispered hint, do so, but do not make a big issue! The young guests probably are unaware and your nagging would only cause embarrassment.

Party Countdown

Pre-party preparations should allow you more time for the birthday child on his special day. To prevent a last-minute rush to get everything completed, refer to the following time schedule for help in planning and executing party preparations.

Time	Completed
2 Weeks Before Party	
Decide on party theme	☐
Decide where to have the party	☐
Make a guest list	☐
Determine construction materials and supplies needed	☐
1½ Weeks Before Party	
Make and deliver invitations	☐
1 Week Before Party	
Order cake from bakery (if not making it yourself)	☐
Buy film and flashbulbs for camera	☐
Purchase party favors and supplies	☐
Purchase birthday present from family	☐
Construct decorations, name cards, etc.	☐
Invite someone to help with party	☐

2 Days Before Party
    Organize a room or area where party will be held. ☐
    Rearrange furniture, put away breakables, mow lawn or whatever... ☐
    Practice party manners ☐

1 Day Ahead
    Prepare party foods ☐
    Prepare cake (if not buying it) ☐
    Assemble items needed for games and activities ☐
    Plan the schedule of events for party (see below) ☐
    Make a note of a few alternate activities that might be needed ☐
    Put up decorations ☐

Day of the Party
    Arrange time to discuss the anticipated party events with your child ☐
    Get house ready (keep housework to a minimum). Sweep floors,
      but don't waste time mopping and waxing. Spills during party are almost guaranteed. ☐
    Assign "get ready" tasks to each family member ☐
    Make a final check:
      Materials for activities are assembled ☐
      Decorations are up ☐
      Table is ready ☐
      There is a place for gifts ☐
      Plenty of coat hangers are in front closet ☐
      Waste basket or a box is available for disposing wrapping paper and other scraps ☐
      Pan of water, paper towels and waste basket are available
       (this will minimize bathroom lineup when children need to wash hands
       before cooking and eating) ☐
      Plenty of paper sacks are available so that guests can easily
       carry favors and prizes home ☐

The Party

Activity	Approximate Time

Greeting:
    Place a smile on your face and use a soft voice.
    Help child to open door and greet arrivals.
    Introduce children to each other.   10-15 minutes

Warm Up Activity:
    Assign helper to lead an activity while you
    and birthday child greet guests.   10-15 minutes

Games and Activities:
    If prizes are awarded, make sure each child wins something.
    Be sure games are not all based on the most competent winning.
    Let games rules be flexible.   30-60 minutes

Be alert to signals that children are ready for different kind of activity.
Alternate quiet games with more active ones.
Make sure all of the children are included and enjoy themselves.

Birthday Table — 15-30 minutes

Opening Presents — 10-15 minutes

Getting Ready for Home:
Have children involved in an activity similar to arrival activities while they wait for parents or for host to drive them home. — 10-15 minutes

After the Party

When the last child has left, look around. Signs of the party will be everywhere. There will be cake crumbs on the table, wrapping paper scraps on the floor, and half-inflated balloons still hanging from the lights.

Mom and dad, hug the birthday child, tell him how much you love him and how proud you are of him. Remember to thank the other children for their help. Now take the time to relax. Sit down, put your feet up and close your eyes. While resting review the thousand and one reasons why you are lucky to be a parent.

All family members will need time to unwind. The birthday child may enjoy quietly looking at his gifts or taking a nap and brothers and sisters also may choose to do something quiet alone. All have worked very hard to help make the party a success.

Later, at dinner or before going to bed when everyone has had time to relax, the family can gather and discuss the special events, with all sharing what they enjoyed most. Now is a good time to present the family gift.

The party's over, but the family will remember the planning, preparation and sharing time as well as the good time had by all at the party. Congratulations on a job well done!

Do not be in a rush to put the house in tip top shape. Just do what is absolutely necessary. Tomorrow, when you are not so tired, will be soon enough for mopping the floor or vacuuming the rug. So they can be enjoyed longer, plan to leave the decorations up for a few days.

1
Birthdays with Friends

Clown Birthday Party

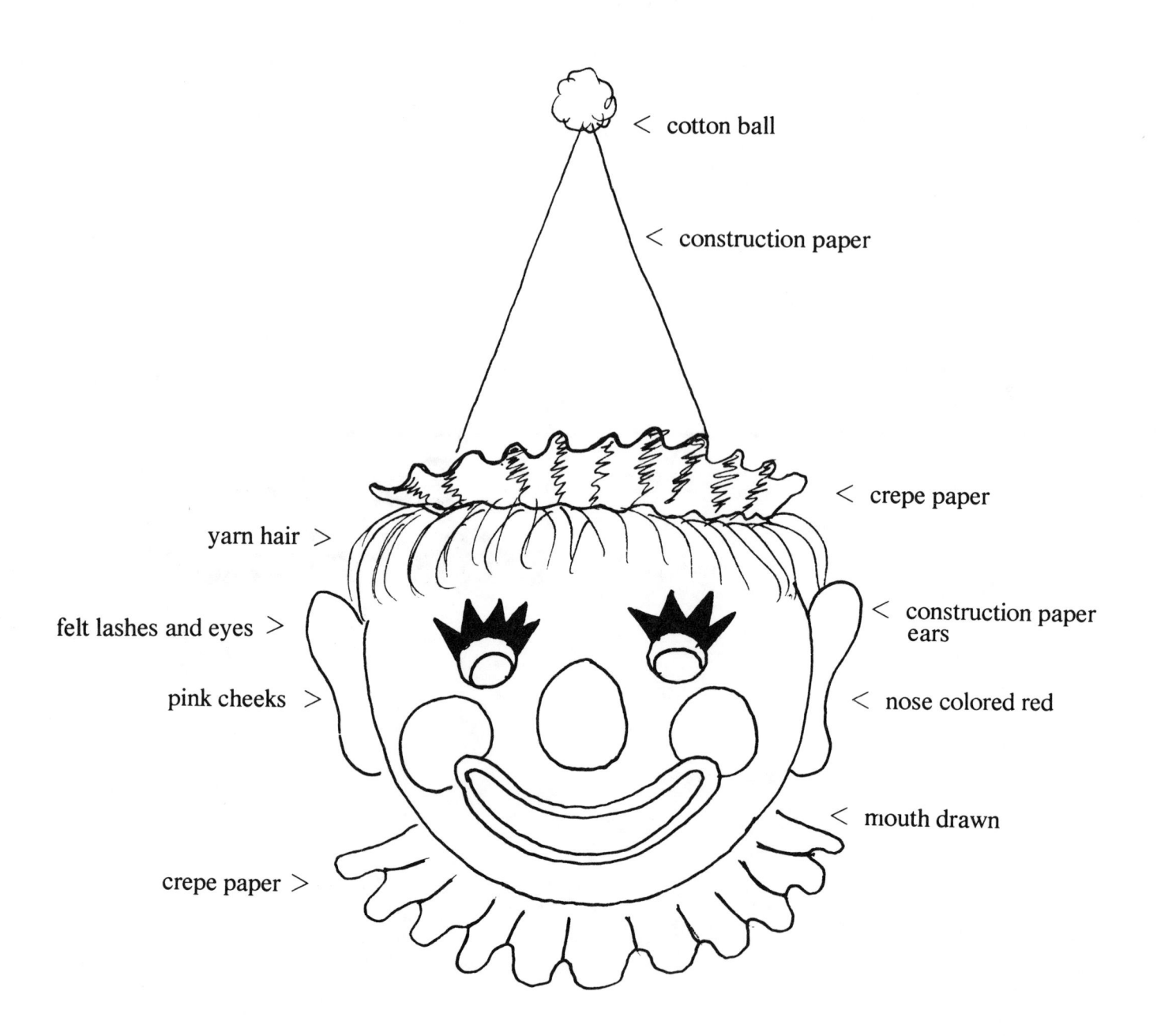

< cotton ball

< construction paper

< crepe paper

yarn hair >

felt lashes and eyes >

pink cheeks >

crepe paper >

< construction paper ears

< nose colored red

< mouth drawn

Clown Birthday Party

Ages: 3-7 years

Invitations:

A brightly colored face of a clown pasted on folded piece of construction paper.

Decorations:

Clown Faces — Paint faces on balloons with magic markers. Add hats made with crepe or construction paper. Hang from light fixtures or attach to hooks on walls with string.

Clown Place Mats — Birthday child and guests make clown pictures on 12-by-18-inch construction paper.

Tent — Create effect by hanging streamers of crepe paper from center fixture to chairs around party table.

Menu and Recipes:

Melon Boat — Mix honeydew, cantalope, or watermelon balls with seedless grapes and 1 large can of fruit cocktail. Serve in half of scooped out cantalope or watermelon.

Clownwiches — Cut circles out of slices of bread. Use leftover corners of bread as triangle hats and collars. Melt cheese on bread or spread bread pieces with peanut butter, cream cheese, cottage cheese, or other favorite spread. Have grated American cheese, pickle slices, olive slices, cut pimento, and orange and apple slices in small dishes on table. Each child uses his imagination to create a face on his clownwich.

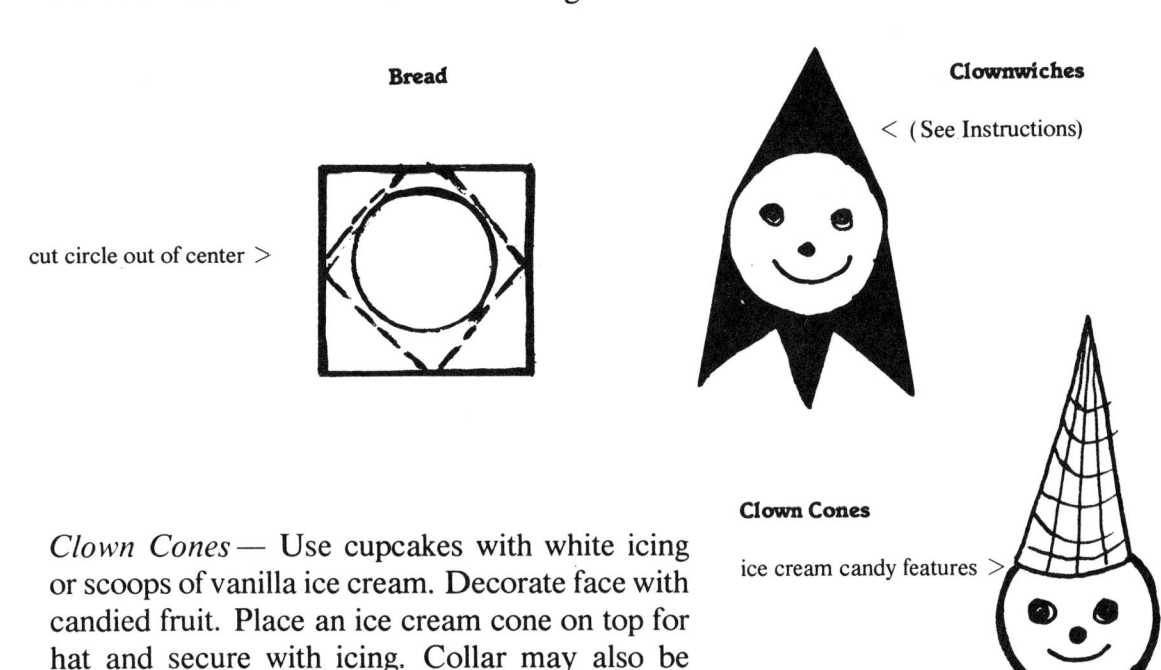

Bread

cut circle out of center >

Clownwiches

< (See Instructions)

Clown Cones — Use cupcakes with white icing or scoops of vanilla ice cream. Decorate face with candied fruit. Place an ice cream cone on top for hat and secure with icing. Collar may also be made with icing. If ice cream is used, keep in freezer until ready to serve.

Clown Cones

ice cream candy features >

Clown Cakes — Bake one 8-inch round cake. Frost with white icing. Make lines for the clown face by poking the frosting with a toothpick first. Follow toothpick lines with colored icing. Red licorice candy is good for hair, candy cherries can be used for nose and raisins can be the eyes. Make hat, ears, and collar out of construction paper and attach to cake head.

Activities:

Arrival — Children may draw clown pictures that will be used as placemats.

Clowns — Assemble old dresses, shirts, pants, shoes, hats, pocketbooks, and jewelry. Each guest may dress up as a clown. If makeup is used on the face, pat a tiny bit of vaseline on first — it makes it easier to remove makeup.

Parade of Clowns — After children have completed their costumes play a jolly march record and have a clown parade. Award prizes for the funniest, tallest, shortest, fattest, etc. Be sure that each clown receives a prize.

Pin the Nose on the Clown — Draw a clown's face but put only an X where the nose should be. Make circles out of red construction paper. Put a double row of tape on back of each circle. Each child gets a turn to be blindfolded and "Pin the Nose on the Clown."

Clown Toss — Collect an old refrigerator box. Paint a clown's face on one side. Cut out spaces for eyes, nose, top of hat and at sides of mouth. Children try to throw bean bags into holes. If children are older, instead of a "clown face" paint a clown's body on box and cut out a large circle where the head should be. Any child who wishes may have a turn to go inside the box and be the clown. The clown sticks his head out of the hole and makes faces or tells funny jokes. Other children try to hit him with small soft Nerf balls.

Look at the Funny Clown — The child who is the clown stands about 20 to 30 feet in front of the other children. He makes funny faces and does funny tricks while other children approach him skipping or walking and chanting "Look at the funny clown!" When they are quite near the clown says, "Boo!" and chases them back to the starting line. A new clown is picked and the game is repeated.

Clowns in a Row — Make about five clown faces. Hold upright with a triangle paper stand. Place the clowns in a row on a table edge. The player stands at least five feet away from the table and tries to knock the clowns over with Nerf balls or bean bags.

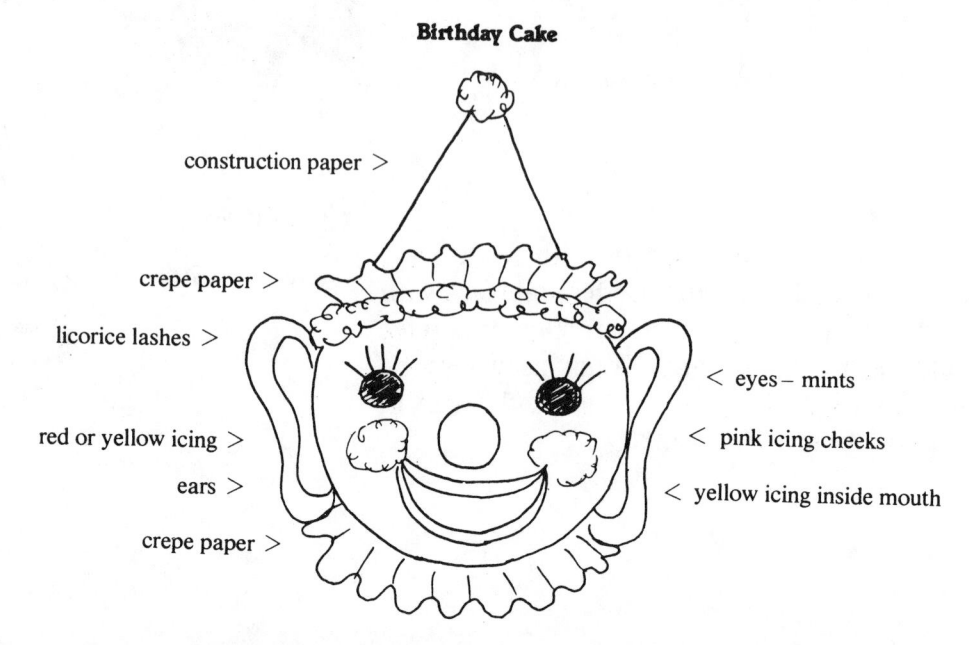

Birthday Cake

construction paper >
crepe paper >
licorice lashes >
red or yellow icing >
ears >
crepe paper >

< eyes – mints
< pink icing cheeks
< yellow icing inside mouth

Mouse Birthday Party

Mouse Birthday Party

Ages: 3-6 years

Invitations:

A slice of cheese or mouse figure. (See Introduction, Preparation for a Party).

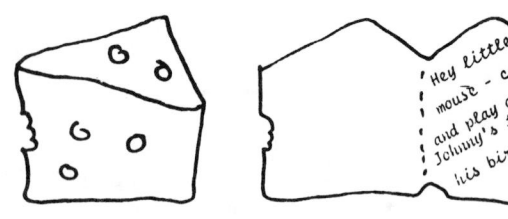

Enlarge four times for invitation

Decorations:

Door — Make a child-sized mouse by enlarging the illustration provided or drawing around outline of child, then adding ears, tail, etc.

Cheese House — Obtain a large box from a furniture store. Paint the box a light orange with tempera. (Liquid starch added to paint will help it stick.) Cut circular holes in the box. Make small holes for peeking and a large one for crawling in or out of house.

Tunnel — Arrange chairs in two parallel rows. Cover with a sheet.

Hideaway — Cover a card table with a sheet.

Cat and Mouse Silhouettes — Enlarge patterns, place on wall.

Table Centerpiece — A stuffed toy mouse or duplicate cut-out of illustrated mouse.

Mouse Placemats — Decorate 12-by-18-inch paper with ink print mouse pictures as described below.

Mouse Place Cards — Each child presses thumb into ink pad, then stamps print on card twice to make mouse ears. Add a nose, eyes, and whiskers with a marker. Label each child's name plus the word Mouse (Susan Mouse).

Mouse Ears — Use 6-inch paper plates. Mouse ears (half circles of brown paper) can be attached at the top. At bottom attach piece of brown yarn to represent a tail.

Favors at each place might be cat and mouse erasers found at variety stores.

Mouse Place Cards and Placemats

Menu:

Mouse Cupcakes

Nibble Foods — Bite sizes of crackers or cereal, cheese, carrots, celery, or apples.

Fruit Drink — Apple juice

Mouse Cupcakes — Make devils' food cupcakes. Cover with yellow frosting. Ears are mints cut in half. Eyes are M & Ms and nose is corn candy.

Activities:

Mouse Ears, Face, and Tail — Cut strip of brown paper long enough to reach around a child's head. Each child cuts out ears from brown paper, which are then stapled or pasted into place on paper strip. Draw whiskers on face with eyebrow pencil. Tails can be made by stuffing one leg of hose with newspapers or strips of cloth. Fasten to clothes with safety pin. Invite children to wear leotards or pajamas so they will look like mice.

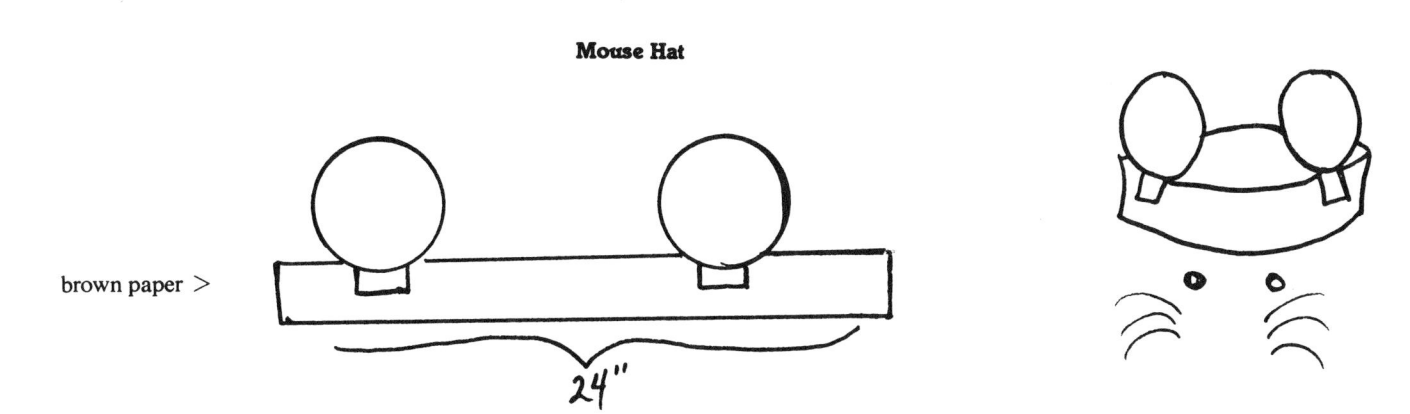

Mouse Hat

brown paper >

24"

Nibble Hunt — Discuss how little mice are always looking for something to nibble. Suggest that since they are dressed to look like mice they too should search for nibble food. Provide each with a small brown sack with his name printed on side. Children search in party room for hidden nibble food. (Candy, cookies, etc. covered with cellophane.)

Mousetrap — Make a mousetrap by having two children hold hands to form tunnel. Others, pretending to be mice, crawl under tunnel while leader chants, "Creep through the mousetrap." At words, "Close the mousetrap," the tunnel closes and a mouse is caught! Trapped mice can then become part of another mousetrap. Continue until all the mice are caught.

Three Blind Mice — Song:
"Three blind mice, three blind mice.
See how they run. See how they run.
They all ran after the farmer's wife
Who cut off their tails with a butcher knife.
Did you ever see such a sight in your life as Three Blind Mice?"

Dramatize song. Three children who are mice (with tails) pretend to chase the farmer's wife. The farmer's wife then turns around and chases them and tries to hit their tails with rolled up newspaper.

Tip the Cat — Draw five cats and place on ledge or table. To play, a child stands about five feet away from cats and tries to hit them with a Nerf ball.

Tip the Cat

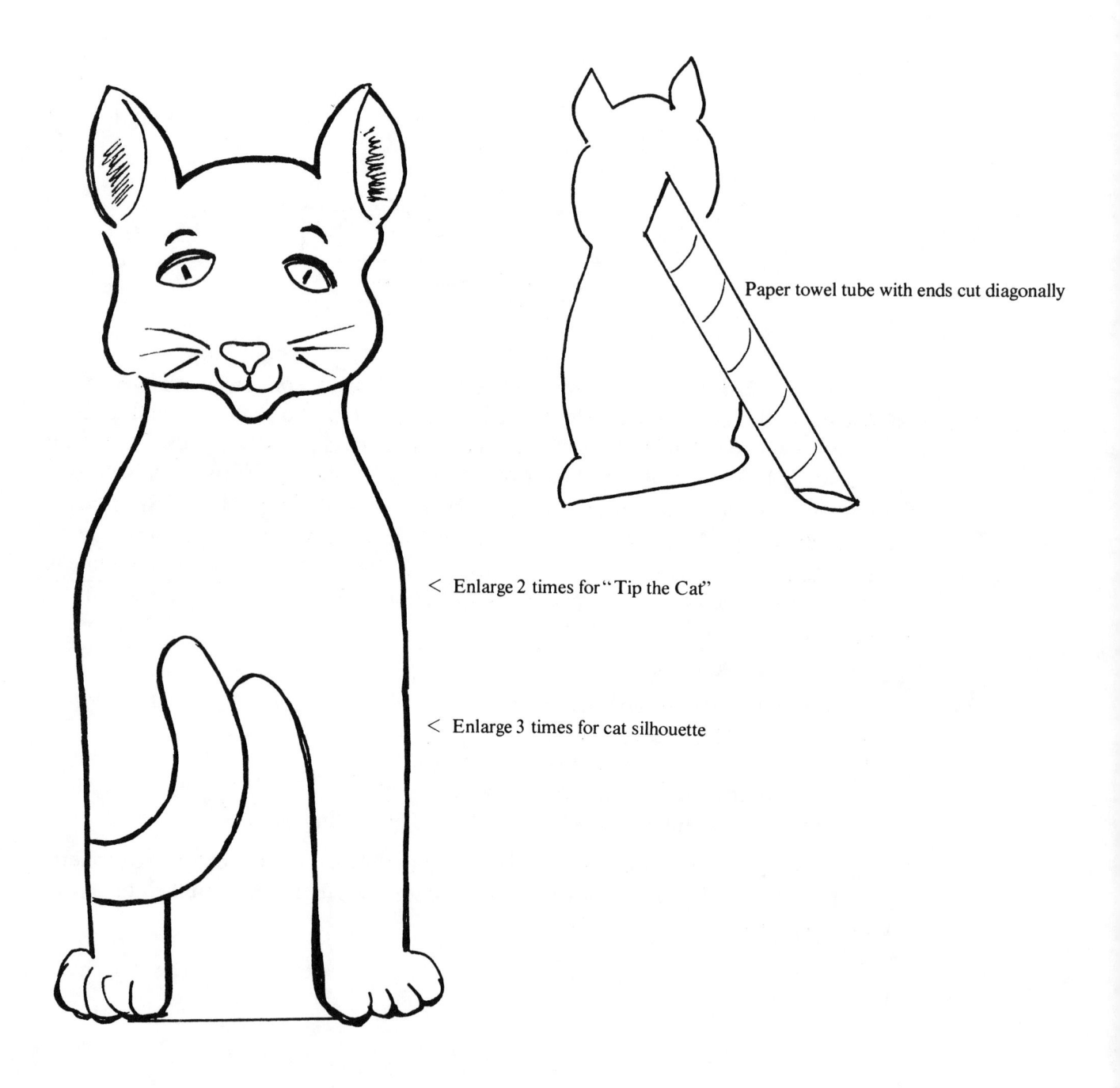

Paper towel tube with ends cut diagonally

< Enlarge 2 times for "Tip the Cat"

< Enlarge 3 times for cat silhouette

Puppet Birthday Party

Decorate as you like!

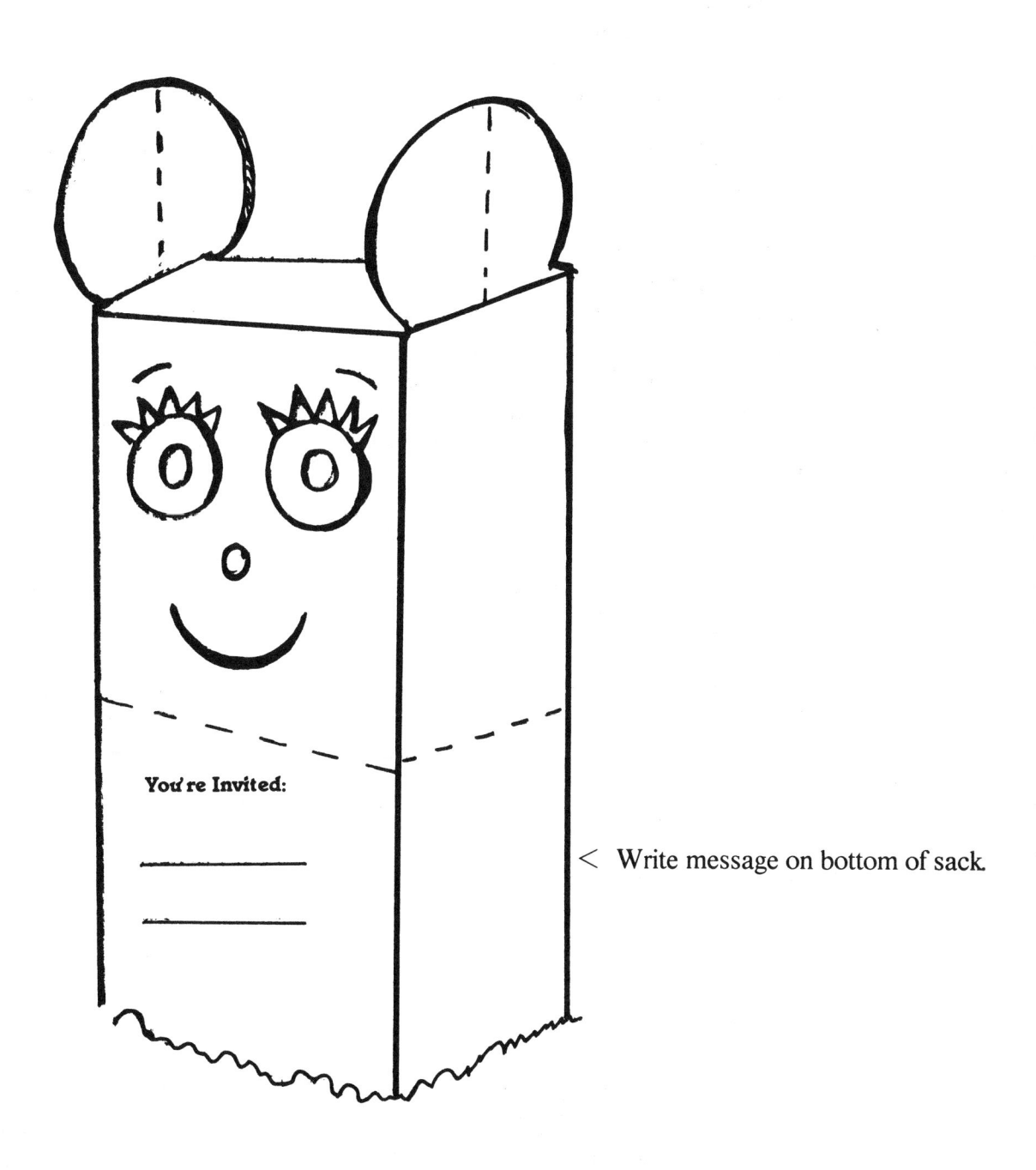

< Write message on bottom of sack.

You're Invited:

Puppet Birthday Party

Ages: 3-6 years

Invitations:
Puppet made out of small paper sack. Place message on back. If mailed, fold and place in envelope.

Decorations:
Hang on walls cardboard puppets, real puppets or use child's dolls by attaching strings to head, hands, and feet. At the table use the cake as a centerpiece. Make place card puppets with popsicle stick, clay, and small Styrofoam ball (see illustration).

Place Card Puppets

(illustration: puppet with popsicle stick, paper skirt with name "JENNY", and clay base)

Menu and Recipes:
Stick Puppet Salad— Assemble cheese, celery, carrot sticks, cracker, and slices of banana for body, arms, and legs. Peach halves or pineapple rings can be used for head. Arrange on lettuce leaf. Raisins, marshmallows, small pieces of candy, etc. can be used for face and buttons. Be creative!

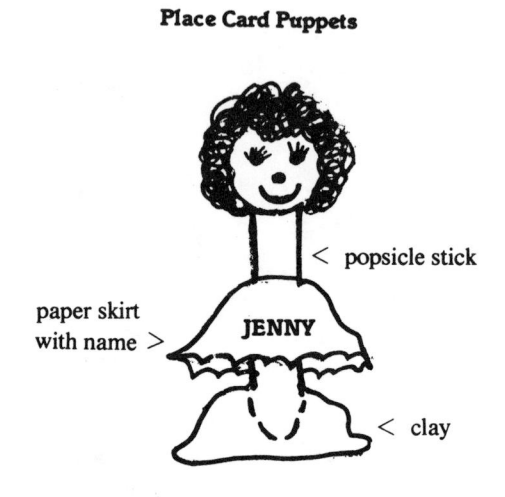

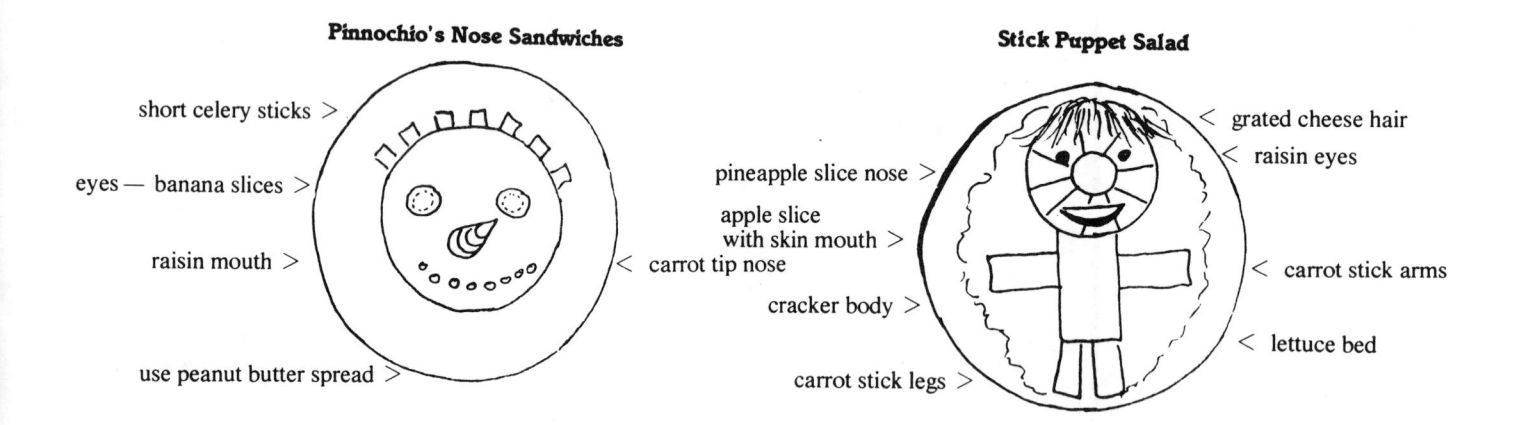

Pinnochio's Nose Sandwiches
- short celery sticks
- eyes — banana slices
- raisin mouth
- use peanut butter spread
- carrot tip nose

Stick Puppet Salad
- pineapple slice nose
- apple slice with skin mouth
- cracker body
- carrot stick legs
- grated cheese hair
- raisin eyes
- carrot stick arms
- lettuce bed

Pinnochio's Nose Sandwiches — Use large glass or biscuit cutter to cut circles out of bread slices. Spread with a variety of spreads: cream cheese, pimento cheese, peanut butter, cottage cheese, etc. Stand carrot, banana, or pickle tips (about 1½ to 2 inches) in middle of circle for nose. Use raisins, marshmallows, apple slices, etc. for nose, eyes, and mouth. (For a real treat, let children decorate their own Pinnochio's Nose Sandwiches).

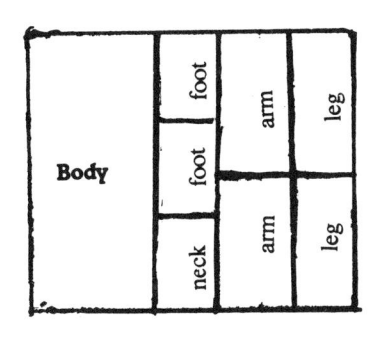

Puppet Cake — Use one 8-inch round layer and one rectangular sheet pan. Cut out rectangular layer for the head as illustrated. Put together pieces of cake to form puppet figure. Ice and decorate.

Activities:

Arrival — As guests arrive they may assemble a puppet using small paper bags, paste, yarn scraps or fabric, or paper and buttons.

Puppet Parade — Invite all puppets with owners to march around the room to music. Award prizes for the funniest, the saddest, the biggest, etc. Make sure each puppet is awarded for some distinctive feature.

Puppet Show — Drape a sheet over two chairs or a table. Children may take turns standing behind the stage. Each child holds a puppet above the sheet and has it perform by singing, telling a favorite story, or moving to a rhythmic record.

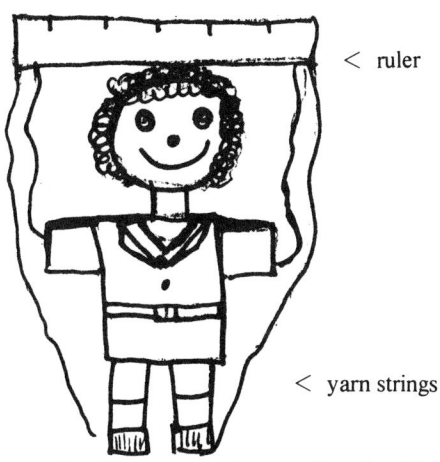

Puppets for Show

< ruler

< yarn strings

Pinnochio's Story — Select from the library a picture book, filmstrip, or movie about Pinnochio. This activity could be during a quiet time before refreshments are served.

Pinnochio's Whale — One child who pretends to be a whale sits in a ring on the floor. Other children pretending to be Pinnochio and his friends swim near him. Without leaving his place in the ring the whale tries to tag one of the players. Places are exchanged when a player is caught.

Puppet Fishing Game — Provide pictures of familiar TV puppet characters (these can be cut out of an inexpensive picture book, then pasted on poster board squares), paper clips, a large box, sticks, string, and magnets. Put a paper clip on each square before placing it in the fishing box. Make fishing poles out of sticks, string, and magnets. Give each child a pole to use for "fishing." The child goes fishing, then names the picture of whom he caught before throwing it back into box. Continue until each child has caught several characters. At the end of the game pictures can be given to children as favors.

Puppet Bingo — Provide bingo cards made with familiar puppet characters. Place eight pictures on each card. Provide children with buttons or beans as markers. Follow rules for regular Bingo, substituting character names for numbers. When a child calls "Bingo" he gets the prize.

Who Am I? — Provide pictures of familiar TV puppet characters and place in a paper sack. Each child takes a turn to pick out a picture. He then acts out the character. The other children try to guess whom he is portraying.

Teddy Bear Picnic

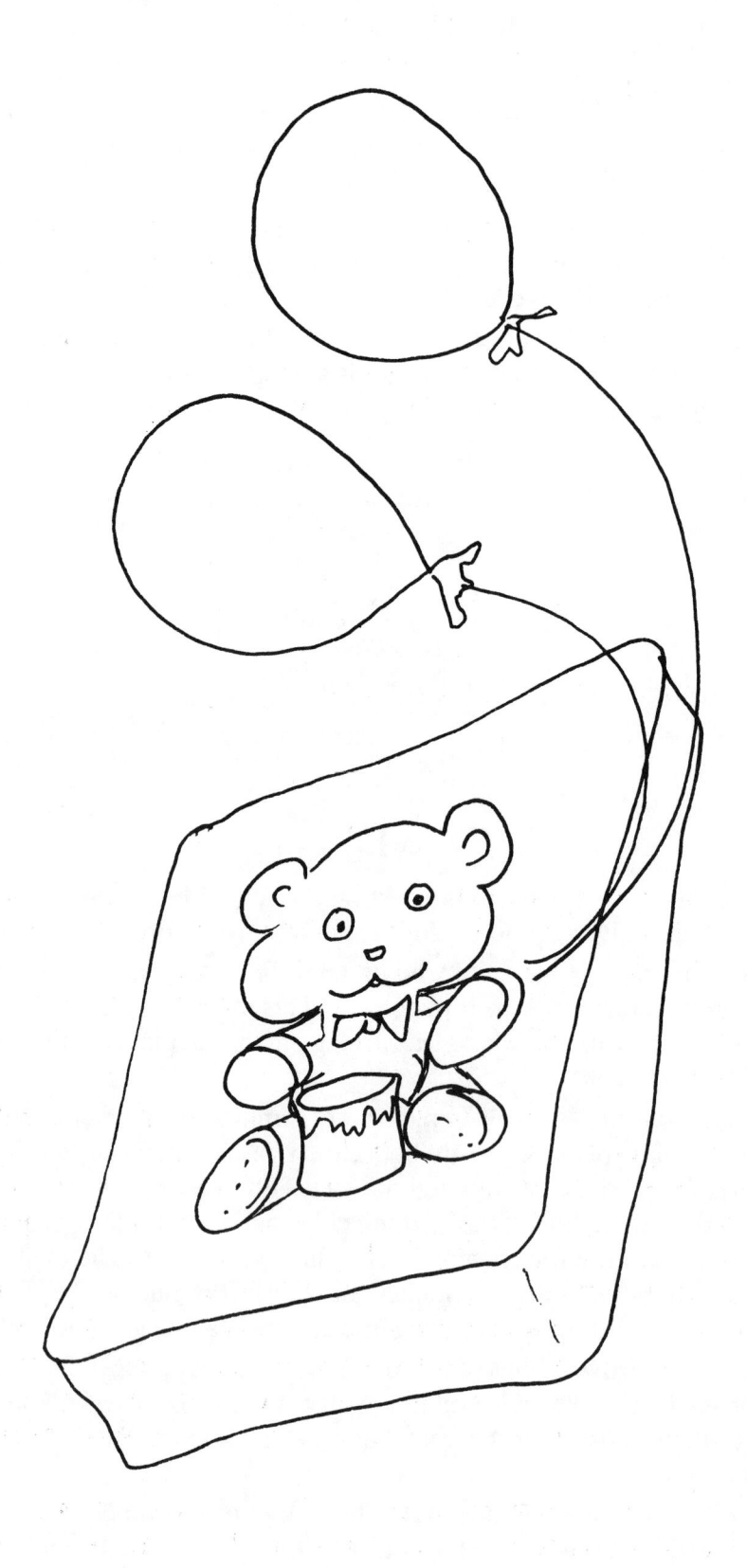

Teddy Bear Picnic

Ages: 4-7 years

Invitations:

Make an outline of a teddy bear holding a honey pot. Write the message inside the lid of the honey pot.

Decorations:

Table — Make place cards by tracing honey pots onto a folded piece of paper. Cut out and write the child's name on side. Glue to a nut cup that is filled with goodies.

Centerpiece — Make a small papier-mache bee hive. On outside of hive attach bees with glue or pipe cleaners. Make or buy pom-pom teddy bears and stand them around hive. Have enough bears and bees to serve as favors for each child.

Placemats — Make a large bear claw out of brown paper.

Room — Attach bee hives, bees, and teddy bears made with construction paper to the ends of crepe paper streamers. Hang streamers over table and around room.

Menu and Recipes:

Clawwiches — Cut out bread circles using a biscuit cutter or glass. Use a rolling pin to slightly change the shape to resemble a claw. Cover claw with peanut butter that has been mixed with 1 tablespoon of honey. Place three peanut halves at the top to represent toenails.

Honey Salad

1 (3 oz.) package orange Jello	1 (11 oz.) jar mandarin oranges, drained
1 cup boiling water	1 (8 oz.) can crushed pineapple, drained
1 pint of orange sherbet	1 cup miniature marshmallows

1 (9 oz.) carton whipped topping

Pour jello into mixing bowl and add boiling water, stirring until jello is dissolved. Add orange sherbet and stir until it is melted. Chill until partly set. Add oranges, pineapple and marshmallows.

Next fold in whipped topping and pour into mold. Refrigerate until set.

Honey Dip

Serve celery and carrot sticks with golden tinted yogurt.

Lemon-Honey Punch

¾ cup lemon juice   6 cups milk

6 tablespoons of honey

Pour all ingredients into a bowl. Beat until it is foamy. Taste. Add more honey if needed. Pour into glasses and serve.

Teddy Bear Cake— Use Anna's Favorite Cake recipe found in the appendix. Decorate as illustrated.

Activities:

Arrival— Children make bear ears by cutting circles out of brown construction paper, then stapling them to butcher paper strips. Wear ears during the party.

Bees Fly Home— Provide each child with five clothes pins decorated to look like bees. (See illustration.) Designate a dishpan or box as a bee hive. Set the hive in the center of an area with boundary line identified with a rope circle. Each child tries to see how many bees he can toss into the hive. To make the game more difficult, enlarge the circle.

Buzz Off— Divide the children into two groups. One group selects a child (probably the birthday child) to be the Head Buzzer. The children in this group form a ring around the Head Buzzer and do their best to protect him from the invading bees. The other bees swarm around the circle. When successfully penetrating the circle they capture the Head Buzzer and take him to their circle. The roles of the two groups are then reversed.

Bee Hive— Make a bee line for each child by pasting egg cups, the number of cups equal to the letters of his name, to a strip of yellow poster paper. Write on cells (yellow circles) the letters of each child's name. Add these and a few cells with bee pictures, after placing a paper clip on each, into the box designated as a hive. Provide a fishing pole, a stick with a piece of string and magnet, for each child. At the signal "go," each child fishes for the letters in his name. If he catches a letter that fits, it is placed in his line in correct sequence. If the letter is one he cannot use he must throw it back in the hive. If a cell with a bee is caught the child must wait until someone else gets another bee before throwing his back in hive and fishing again. Younger children may need to have their names preprinted on the bee line so that the task is to match letters. For fairness, abbreviate long names or use nickname and for very short names add the middle name or initial.

The Bears and the Bees— Prepare several honey pots with plastic cartons and make bees with yellow construction paper backed with masking tape rings. Children divide into two groups — bees and bears. The bees stand inside a "hive," which is identified by a rope circle, and bears sneak around hive. The object of the game is for the bears to try to steal as many honey pots as possible from the hive without being stung by a paper bee. The masking tape ring makes it easy to identify a bear that was stung.

Dancing Bears— On brown butcher paper produce bear claws. Place a ring of masking tape on bottom of each, then stick to the floor or rug in patterns. Children follow the patterns of claws by steps, jumps, and hops. A record such as "Teddy Bear's Picnic" will add a pleasant background.

Dancing Bears

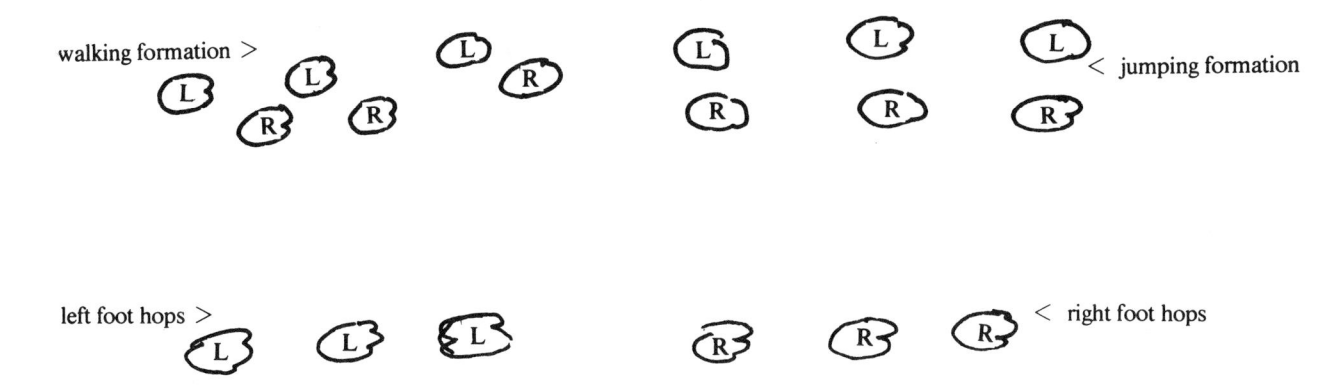

walking formation >   　　　　　　　　　　　　　　　　　　< jumping formation

left foot hops >　　　　　　　　　　　　　　　　　　　　< right foot hops

What Time Is It, Mr. Bee? — Establish a safe home base. Choose a leader to be Mr. Bee. Children follow behind the leader chanting the question, "What time is it, Mr. Bee?" Mr. Bee replies various times such as one-thirty, two o'clock or seven-fifteen. The children continue to chant the same question until Mr. Bee replies, "Dinnertime!" Everyone runs for home because Mr. Bee will try to sting as many as possible. Choose a new Mr. Bee and repeat the game.

Come as a Bum

Come as a Bum

Ages: 4-7 years

Invitations:

Use the bum picture for invitation or write invitation message on the backside of an old can label.

Decorations:

Table — A sturdy box such as one from an appliance store, can serve as a table. Cover the table with an old tattered sheet. Invite each child to decorate his place by drawing a picture on the sheet. (At the end of the party placemats can be torn out and sent home with guests).

Centerpiece — A small campsite complete with shanty and a campfire made with sticks and crepe paper fire.

Sit Upons — Fold several sections of newspapers and stack.

Room — Cover furniture with sheets or push back so it is not noticeable.

Menu and Recipes:

Beany Weenies — Add sliced hot dogs to a can of baked beans. Heat and serve in clean tin cans (tuna fish or other single serving cans work well).

Blops — Make favorite biscuit recipe and add ¼ cup of milk. Drop onto cookie sheet using a serving spoon. Bake until done and serve with butter.

Garbage Can Toss — Serve a tossed salad from a #10 can that has been decorated to look like a garbage can.

Bum Cupcake — Use your favorite cake recipe or the one found in the appendix. Use the preceding picture and follow directions in appendix for decorating the cake.

Activities:

Arrival — Each child is provided with a box to be decorated to resemble a shanty. When shanties are completed place around the room for decoration or use in games.

Musical Shanties — Place shanties in a circle. Each child stands in front of his shanty. Before music starts one child removes his shanty from the circle. Play like "Musical Chairs" by marching around circle, then standing in front of a shanty each time music stops.

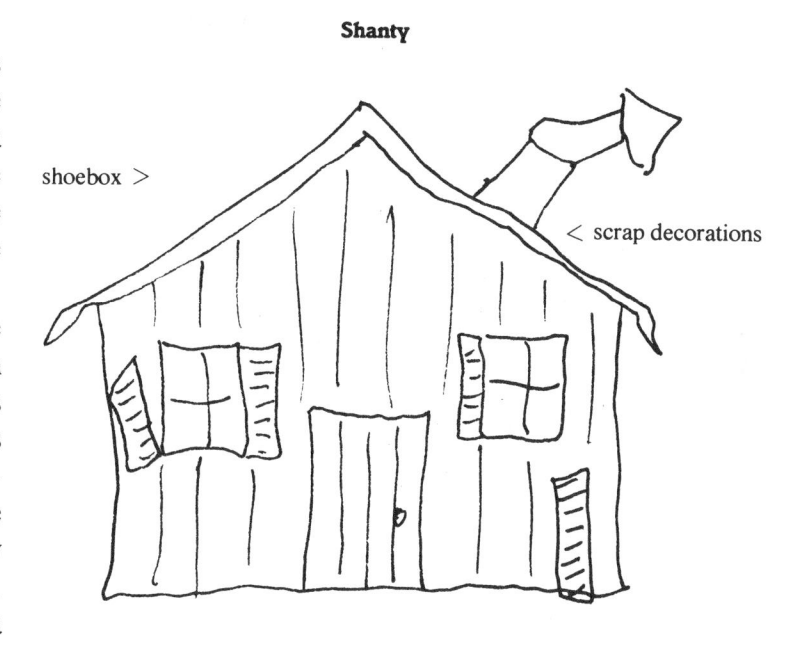

Shanty

shoebox >

< scrap decorations

After each sequence remove one shanty; ask child who did not reach a shanty to leave circle. (They can still be a part by clapping to the music). Continue until one child and one shanty are left.

Bandana Bumble — Wrap items such as a key, spoon, block, comb, brush, eraser, etc. in a piece of cloth and then tie each bandana to a stick. (Make at least three more bandana bundles than number of children playing). Place the bandana bundles in a basket with the sticks pointed up. Assign each child an item to retrieve from the basket. At the "go" signal each child selects a bandana bundle and pulls it out of basket. By feeling he decides if it contains the object he is to find. If choice is incorrect replace bandana bundle in basket and select a new one. If correct item is selected take bandana bundle back to seat and wait until others have finished. Caution players *not* to tell what they feel!

Box Car Jump — Children place sit upons in a train formation. Present each child with a ticket that is a picture or word card of some specific location or landmark (woods, stream, dog house, pond, mountain, orchard, city, etc.). The leader tells a story about a train trip and makes sure to repeat words on cards. Children are to jump up and off their sit upons whenever they hear the name of their ticket. Upon hearing the word "conductor" all children jump up and off their sit upons. Any child who does not follow directions must get off train and return to his shanty. Hint: Adjust the length of the story according to the ages and number of guests at the party. Younger children will benefit by hearing the story first before trying to perform appropriate actions.

Junkyard Jamboree — The day before the party collect construction odds and ends and place in a box. Provide each child with some glue and a large sheet of paper. Invite him to sit in a circle around the box. Before starting each child may select one item to use for constructing a junk collage. At the signal "go" children start up their creation. The rule of the game is children can return to the box as often as needed but can only remove one item at a time. At the end of five minutes put all construction items back into box. Award prizes for the collage that is the most original, the largest, the least likely to exist, etc.

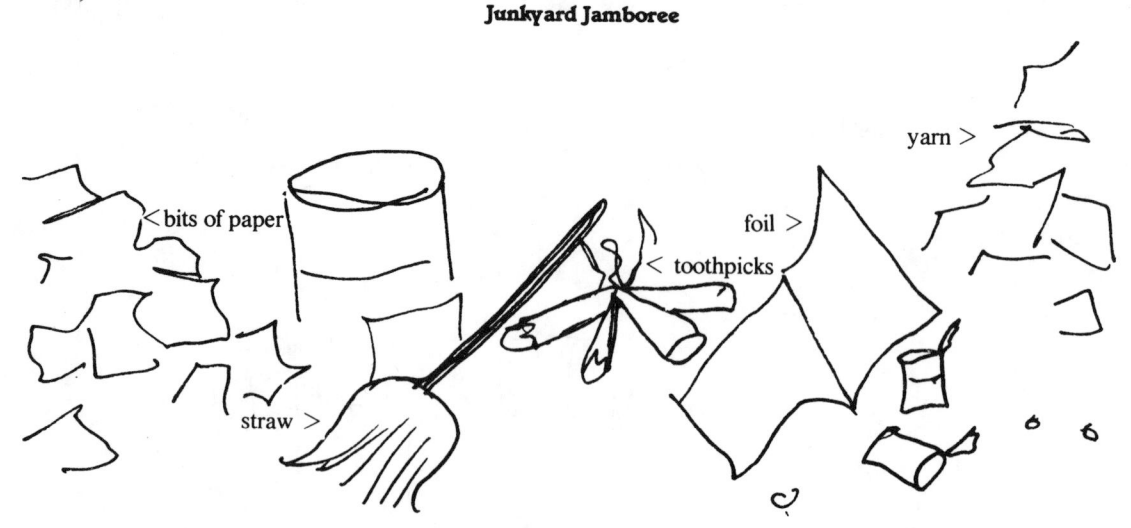

Junkyard Jamboree

Cinderella's Dress Up Birthday Party

Cinderella's Dress Up Birthday Party

Ages: 5-9 years (girls)

Invitations:
Picture of Cinderella in her special gown on front fold of invitation. After picture is drawn and colored, paste on glitter.

Decorations:
Castle — Made out of large boxes and cones, then painted or covered with crepe paper. (If castle is large enough, it can be used as prop for dramatic play).

Room — Pink and white crepe paper streamers hung from light fixtures. Cinderella dolls can be put on display.

Fairy Godmother — Mom dressed up!

Table — Tablecloth, napkins, cups, and plates in pale pastel colors.

Place cards — Tiny mice made with thumb prints (see Mouse Party).

Menu and Recipes:
Tea Sandwiches — Cut favorite sandwiches into small squares.

Cinderella Salad — Make girl figure as illustrated.

Fairy Punch — Gingerale with scoops of strawberry ice cream added.

Cinderella Cake Castle — Use two boxes of white cake mix. Place one box in two rectangle 8-inch pans that have been oiled, dusted with flour, then lined in bottom with wax paper. Place the other cake mix in four 1-pound coffee cans that have been oiled and dusted with flour. Place upright, not touching, in shallow pan for baking. Bake as directed. Cool.

Cinderella Salad
- grated-cheese hair
- raisin eyes
- cinnamon candy lips
- radish
- tomato
- rolled ham slice arms
- lettuce leaf
- black olives

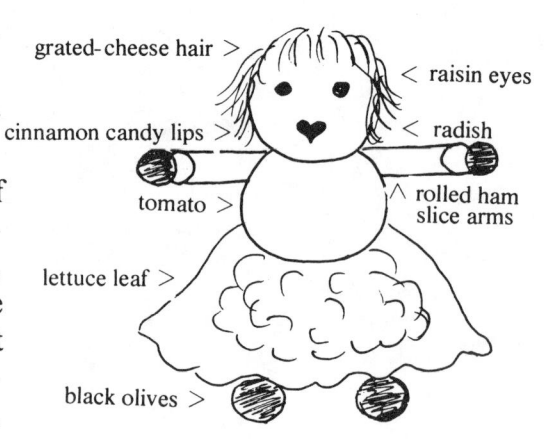

Castle Cake
- pastel frosting
- ice cream cones
- use coffee cans or soup cans

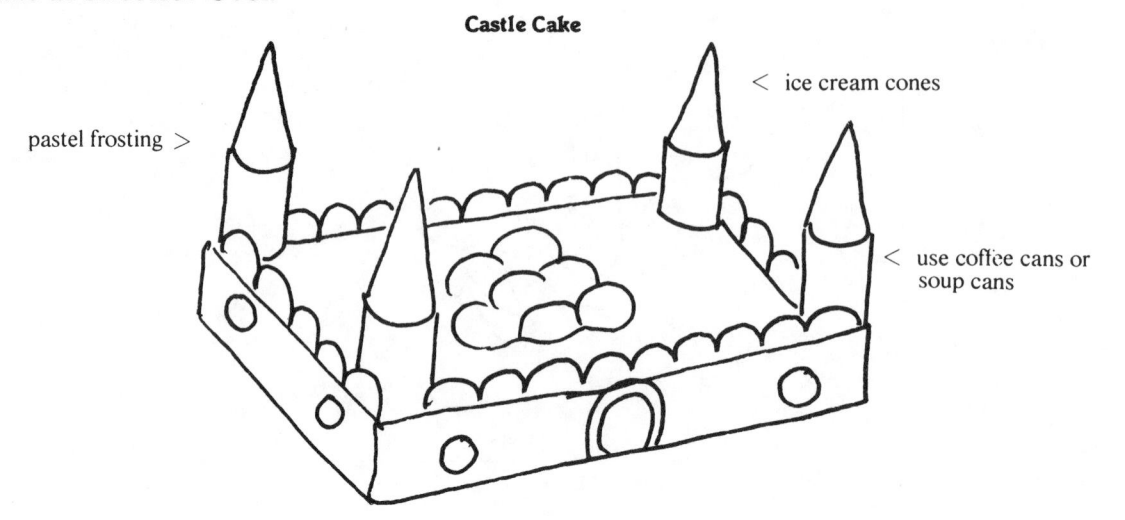

Make a base for cake by covering a cookie sheet with aluminum foil. Place rectangular cakes in middle of base. Frost sides of rectangular cake. Frost the cylinder cakes with a pastel frosting. Place cylinder at each corner of cake. Spread another color of pastel frosting over four sugar ice cream cones. Stand cones upside down on top of cylinders (toothpicks may be needed to secure in place). Using pink frosting and cake decorating tools draw stones, windows, and doors. Complete the door and window decorations with candy-pillow shaped mints. Just before serving make roof by scooping strawberry and vanilla ice cream balls on center of cake.

Activities:

Cinderella Story — Tell the story of Cinderella. (It may be possible to borrow a filmstrip and projector or the book from the local library.) After hearing the story children may dramatize the characters and events.

Hide the Glass Slipper — Choose a child to be Cinderella. All other children sit in a line approximately three feet behind Cinderella. Place a glass slipper behind Cinderella, who pretends to be sleeping. Choose one child to go up and grab the slipper, sit back down in the line, and hide the slipper behind her. All children then chant, "Cinderella, Cinderella, where is your glass slipper?" Cinderella opens eyes and turns around. She gets two guesses as to who took the slipper. If she guesses correctly, that child becomes the new Cinderella. Continue to play until all children have a turn.

Dress Up and Go to the Ball — Assemble make-up, mirrors, hair brushes, combs, pretty bows, ribbons, long skirts, high-heeled shoes, hats, purses, and jewelry. The girls can pretend to be dressing up to go to the ball. When all are dressed in pretty clothes put on a dance record. (Have camera ready).

Clean Away the Cobwebs — Assemble pencils or small brushes, string or yarn, and enough prizes for each child. Before the party run the strings or colored yarn in, out, over, under, and around furniture in party room. Let strings intersect like spider webs in certain areas. Attach one end of the strip to a pencil and the other end to a prize. Children clean away the cobwebs by rolling up their string on a pencil. At the end of the string they find a prize which they may keep.

Shoe Scramble — Children remove their shoes and place in a heap at one end of the party area. They then stand at the starting line at opposite ends of the room. At the "go" signal they must rush to the pile, find their own shoes and put them on correctly. Award a prize to one with shoes on first.

Cinderella's Party Clothes (Memory Game) — Children sit in circle. One child starts the game by naming an article of clothing that Cinderella will wear to the ball. The next child repeats what was said, and adds another article of clothing. Example: Sally says, "Cinderella will wear silver slippers to the ball." Ellen adds, "Cinderella will wear silver slippers and a pink party dress to the ball." Continue all around the circle.

2

Birthday Cooks

A Birthday Stew

A Birthday Stew

Ages: 5-9 years

Invitations:

Black paper folded and cut to resemble a big cooking pot. Include in the message that each guest is to bring a vegetable for the stew.

Decorations:

Room — Fruit and vegetable pictures placed on walls or hung as a mobile from light fixtures. Fill baskets with fruit and vegetables.

Table — A vegetable man centerpiece made by attaching vegetable pieces to each other with toothpicks. Use a white tablecloth. Decorate the green plates and cups with fruit and vegetable stickers.

Place Cards — Cut out fruit and vegetable forms from construction paper, then place human features for face. Try to match the beginning sound of the vegetable with the names of children: Tina Tomato, Paul Potato, etc.

Fruit and Vegetable Favors Out of Clay — Combine 2 cups of flour, 1 cup of salt, and water to moisten. Add water a little at a time and form a ball. Be careful to keep dough from becoming too sticky. Knead dough for 7 to 10 minutes. Store in plastic bag. Make fruits and vegetables out of salt clay. Air dry by placing on a screen, which allows both sides to dry equally well, or bake dry by placing objects on a foil-covered cookie sheet and place in oven set at 350°. Allow one half hour baking time for each ½-inch thickness. Paint with mixture of equal amounts of tempera paint and white glue. Glue a safety pin on back with white glue.

Party Hats — Cut out bands of construction paper. Decorate with construction paper fruits or vegetables or food stickers.

Menu and Recipes:

Birthday Stew

2 lbs. beef chuck, cut into 1½-inch cubes	1 teaspoon Worcestershire Sauce
1 clove of garlic	1 medium onion sliced
1-2 bay leaves	1 tablespoon salt
1 teaspoon sugar	½ teaspoon pepper
½ teaspoon paprika	dash of allspice or cloves

In Dutch oven thoroughly brown meat in shortening. Add 2 cups of hot water and above ingredients. Cover and simmer for 1½ hours, stirring occasionally to keep from sticking. Remove bay leaves and garlic. Add vegetables which children bring and cook 30 to 45 minutes.

Muffins

2 cups of sifted all purpose flour
½ teaspoon salt
1 egg
3 teaspoons of baking powder
2 tablespons sugar.
1 cup milk
¼ cup salad oil

Combine flour, baking powder, salt, and sugar. Beat egg and add 1 cup milk and salad oil. Pour egg, milk, and salad oil at once into dry mixture. Stir quickly. Fill muffin pans that have been lined with paper cups about ⅔ full. Bake 25 minutes at 425°. Serve with butter and jelly.

Birthday Carrot Cake

2 cups sugar
2 teaspoons baking soda
1 teaspoon salt
4 eggs
2 cups of sifted flour
2 teaspoons cinnamon
1⅔ cups salad oil
3 cups grated raw carrots

In a large bowl combine sugar, sifted flour, baking soda, cinnamon, and salt. Add salad oil, slightly beaten eggs and carrots. Bake for 35 minutes in a large loaf pan. Frost with cream cheese frosting.

Nut Cups — Filled with pieces of fresh vegetables.

Vegetable Juice — Have a variety of juices available for refreshments.

Activities:

Cook the Stew — Prior to arrival of children prepare the meat and stock for stew. Place in a kettle or slow cooker. As each child arrives, he/she puts on an apron and washes hands. With adult supervision, the child carefully peels, then cuts up vegetable for the stew.

Muffins — Print the muffin recipe on a large posterboard. Have all ingredients and utensils needed to make muffins on table. Read the recipe with children. Ask children to identify ingredients and cookware. Assign tasks. Reread the recipe, then help each child do his part. The chidren may wish to taste before baking. (As a sanitary precaution provide each child with his own "taster" plate and spoon.)

Treasure Hunt — Collect materials such as old magazines, newpapers, grocery ads and seed catalogues, sheets of paper, scissors, and paste. Give each child a name of a fruit or vegetable to research. Ask him to look in the magazines, grocery ads, and seed catalogs to find as many pictures as possible of his food. As pictures are found, point out that foods are prepared in various ways.

Food Turn Around — Have pictures of fruits and vegetables available. Choose two children to be in center of playing circle. One child hides his eyes while the other child gets a food picture pinned on his back. The object of the game is for the child who closed his eyes to identify the food on the other child's back. This will not be easy because the other child dodges and tries to keep his back turned away from the first child.

Upset Food Basket — Have children sit on chairs in a circle. Pass out food pictures, making sure that the same kind is given to two children. Call out the names of fruits and vegetables. When the two children hear the name of their food they quickly exchange seats. At the signal, "Upset the Food Basket," everyone finds a new chair.

Food Memory Game — Prior to the party, fill a tray with food, then cover with a cloth. Arrange children in a circle around the covered tray. (Be sure each child can see clearly.) At signal, remove cover so children can view the food on tray for about ten seconds. Quickly recover the tray. Give children a pencil and paper. They may either draw a picture of the food they remembered seeing or write the names. The winner gets a prize (perhaps the Big Banana).

Health King and Queen (A Dramatization) — Prior to party make crowns and robes for the health king and queen and cardboard swords for guards and cover two chairs so they resemble throne chairs. Tell the story:

Long ago there was a kingdom called Health. The king and queen who ruled that land liked to have the people come to visit them in their palace. Their only demand was that the visitors must know how to keep healthy. On special visiting days two guards stood outside the palace. As visitors arrived the guards stopped them by crossing their swords. Guards requested the visitors to tell the password of how they kept healthy. Those who said things like "Eating candy" or "Staying up late to watch TV" had to return home. Visitors who said things like "I eat vegetables," "I get plenty of exercise," or "I get plenty of sleep," were invited to enter the castle and visit the king and queen.

Familiar Foods

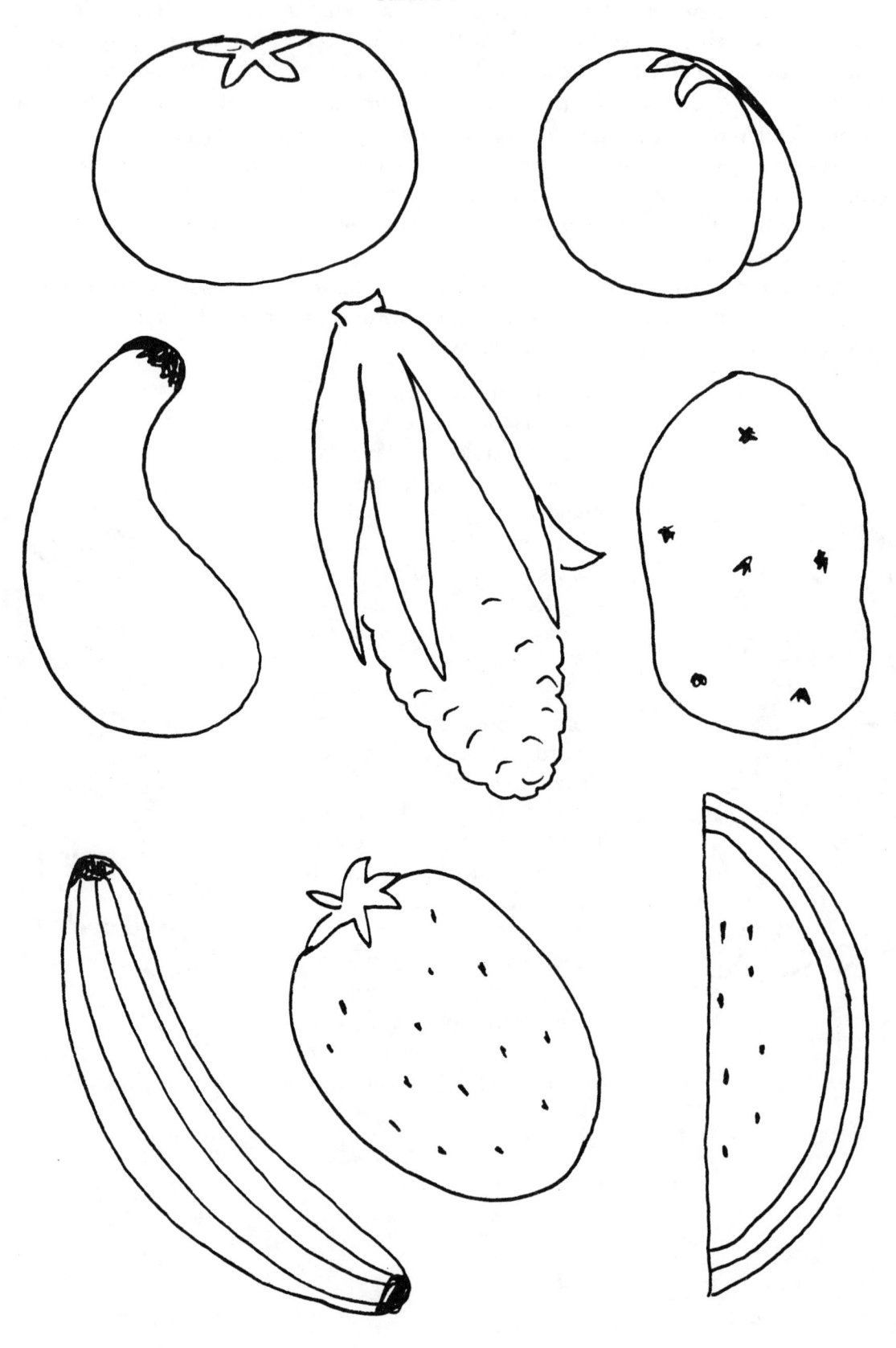

Do It Yourself Birthday Party

Do It Yourself Birthday Party

Ages: 6-10 years

Invitations:

Send guests a folded piece of construction paper with message inside but outside blank. Ask each child to create a card cover and bring it to the party. Award prizes for the funniest, prettiest, most colorful, and silliest. Have extra blank pieces of paper for the child who forgot invitation. Include several categories so that each child wins a prize.

Decorations:

See activities.

Menu and Recipes:

Make Your Own Sandwiches — Prepare cold cuts ahead of time. Have bread, cheese, and spreads out on counter so children can make their own.

Make Your Own Ice Cream —
Freezers: Provide a ½-gallon milk carton cut 3 inches tall, a small 6 oz. frozen juice can, and stirrer or plastic spoon for each child.
Make ice cream mix by beating 3 eggs, then adding 1½ cups of sugar or 1 cup of honey, 4¾ (or 4½ if honey used) cups light cream or half-and-half and 3 tablespoons vanilla to eggs and mixing well.
Have each child ladle 4 oz. (¼ cup) of ice cream mix into a measuring cup and pour it into the juice can. Have him place the can in the center of the milk carton. Then alternately place layers of ice and salt in the carton around the outside of the can. Remind each child to be very careful to avoid getting ice or salt into the ice cream mix. Next, occasionally stir mixture in the can until ice cream is frozen (approximately 15 to 20 minutes).

Make Your Own Sundae — Children add fresh fruit, nuts, or whipped topping to ice cream.

Moo Shake — Child adds 1 tablespoon of jelly to each glass of milk. Stir well before drinking.

Decorate Your Own Cake — Make a cake or cupcakes but do not frost. Assemble frosting and goodies for decorating. Each child will frost and decorate his own piece of cake or cupcake before eating.

Activities:

Decorations — Assemble paper strips, glue, construction paper, crayons, magic markers, plain white table cloth, balloons, etc. As guests arrive they participate in making decorations such as paper chains. Balloons can be blown up and decorated with magic markers, then hung around room. The paper birthday table cloth and place cards can also be decorated by guests.

Write a Birthday Story — Assemble paper, pencils, and crayons. Each child writes or dictates to an adult a short story about the birthday child. The stories can be true or make believe. If children are unsure it may help for an adult to give a starter idea. Each child draws a picture to illustrate his story, and all the stories are shared with the birthday child.

Make a Game — Assemble game cards (four each of three different colors), a box to hold cards, and markers. Write one of the following rules on each card: On red card — pair off, sit in two circles facing each other. On blue cards — use balloons, use balls, use stones, or use oranges. On yellow cards — keep away, spoon pass, pass with no arms, or time stop. Set up rules: If a race, the fastest team wins. If time stop, the winner is the person who is never caught with the object. In keep away, the teams score points for not letting other team obtain object. To play game children form teams. Each team chooses one card of each color and puts them together to form a game. If the guest group is small, they may choose to play each type of a "make your own game."

Penny Pinching — Guests make a target board with areas assigned as goals. Each guest gets five pennies, which are tossed toward target. Award prizes.

Invitations to Play Games — Invite each guest to write on a piece of paper a game he or she would like to play. Place suggestions in a bag. The birthday child reaches into bag and pulls out a paper with a suggestion. If time permits, play several games.

Faces — Children sit in a circle. At the signal, the birthday child turns to the person on his left and makes funny faces in an effort to make that person smile or laugh. If he is able to do so in 15 seconds or less, that person must leave the circle and he continues to make the next person laugh. If his attempt is unsuccessful, the other child turns to the person on his left and attempts to make him laugh. The game continues until just one child remains.

Keep it Going — Put a large piece of paper up on a wall or across the floor. The birthday child is given a magic marker and starts to draw a picture on the paper. Although he may be thinking about a favorite toy, he draws only a short line. The next child is asked to try and figure out what the drawing is and add another line to it. Children keep adding something until an object appears. Then the last children add the finishing touches. After the picture is complete, discuss what each child had in mind as he drew.

3
Birthdays Here and There

Space Wars Birthday

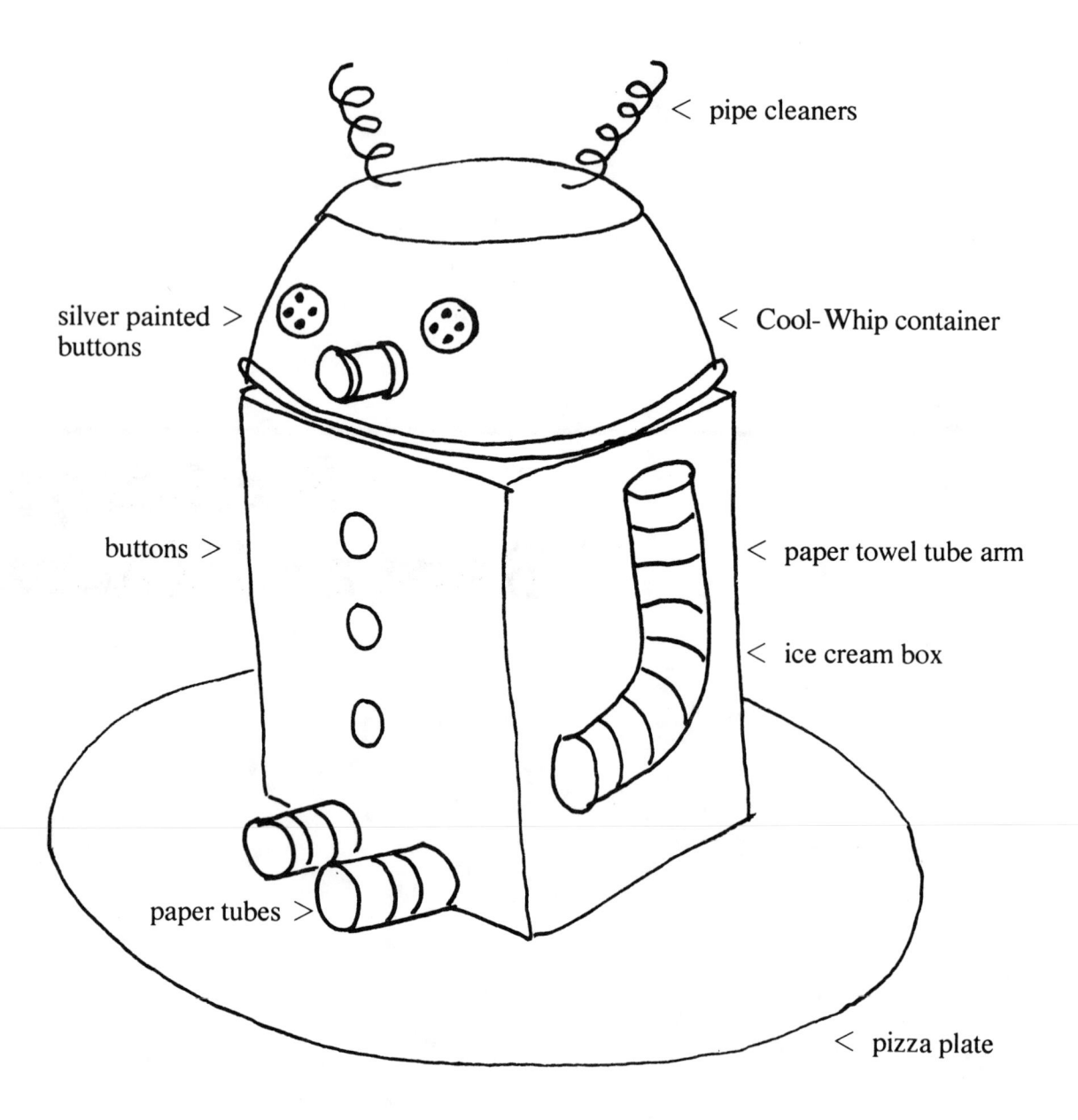

< pipe cleaners

silver painted > buttons

< Cool-Whip container

buttons >

< paper towel tube arm

< ice cream box

paper tubes >

< pizza plate

Paint Alpha Omega with aluminum paint.

Space Wars Birthday

Ages: 5-10 years

Invitations:

An outer space scene. On front fold of invitation the child fills page with patches of bright colors with wax crayon. Cover with film of India ink. Use a sharp tool such as a nail to scrape out designs such as stars, space ships, and plants.

Decorations:

Door — Spaceman form made by tracing around child. Use magic markers or crayons to make features of a space man.

Room — Spaceship made by decorating a large packing box. Make cone top with large circle of heavy butcher paper. Color, then cut to center and overlap to make cone effect. Space mobiles are made by hanging forms of the sun, moon, spaceships, and comets from light fixtures. If foil is used they will reflect bits of light when room is darkened.

Figurines — Commercial space dolls and other dolls dressed to look like space people.

Table — Tablecloth made from white butcher paper. Invite guests to create an outer space scene with crayons or magic markers.

Mars Men Napkins — Use green napkins. In center of each napkin enclose a cotton ball with rubber band or small ribbon. Make mouth and eyes with a ball point pen.

Star-Shaped Blotters — Place under each glass.

Space Plates — Made by pasting stars around the rim of plates.

Space Place Cards — Created with cardboard tubes and paper. For example: stars, moon, etc. On each form have a space name such as Robby Robot, Sally Sun, Juniper Jack, or Mark Mars.

Alpha Omega Robot Centerpiece — Use a Cool-Whip carton as head and a large cardboard ice cream carton as the body. Arms may be made from cardboard cylinders. Build on base of a round pizza cardboard plate. Cover with aluminum paint. Electrical silver tape may be used for outline. Use spools, pipe cleaners, and buttons for features.

Costumes:

Spacemen Masks — Make from 5-gallon ice cream cartons. Paint with aluminum paint or cover with foil. Cut holes for eyes. Draw features. Use pipe cleaners for antennas.

Spaceman Masks

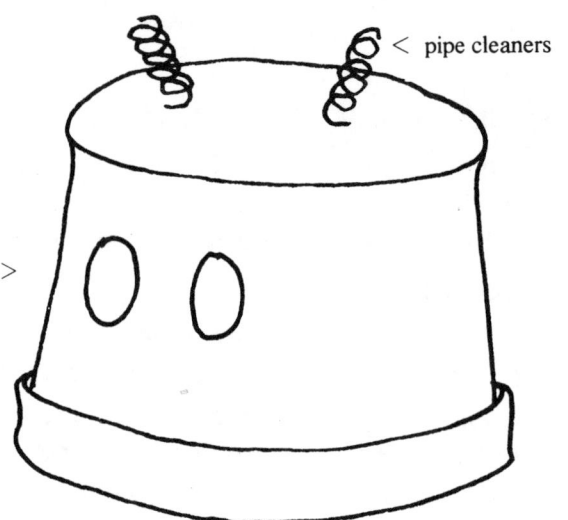

< pipe cleaners

ice cream containers >

Space Vadar Mask

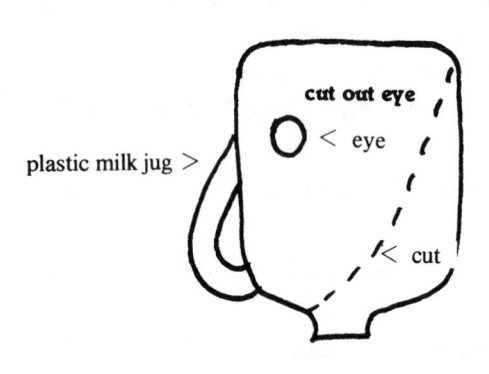

cut out eye
< eye
plastic milk jug >
< cut

Space Suit from Bag

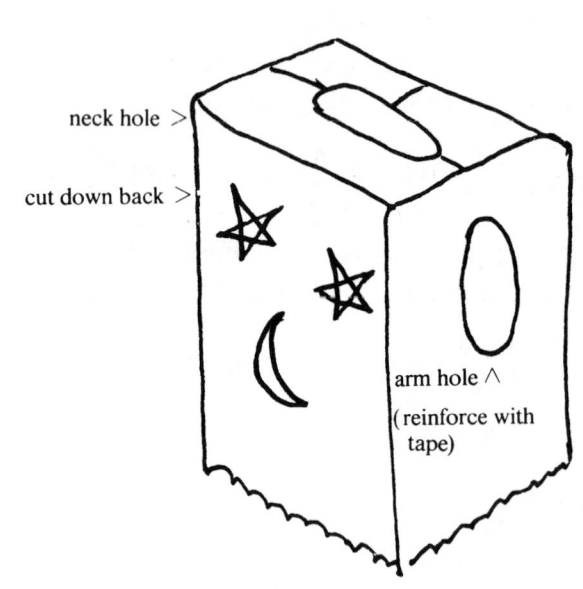

neck hole >
cut down back >
arm hole ∧ (reinforce with tape)

Space Invaders Masks — Can be created with 2-gallon milk jugs. Submerge in hot water to soften, then cut form and eye holes as illustrated. The child holds mask in front of face.

Space Dancer Suits — Can be created out of paper sacks. Cut a neck hole in bottom of large paper sack. Start at center of neck hole and cut down the center of back. Cut arm openings on sides. Reinforce holes with tape. Decorate by drawing space designs. If flourescent crayons are available they will add vividness. Laser Beams may be purchased or created by covering the lens of flashlights with tinted cellophane or tissue paper.

Menu and Recipes:

Space Burgers — Small buns and large hamburgers

Solar Chips — Potato Chips

Lunar Disks — Pickles

Milky Way Pudding — Add green tint to tapioca pudding

U.F.O. Birthday Cake — Use two box cake mixes. Make three layers, two in 8-inch round pan, and one in a 9-inch pan. Frost with easy frosting recipe. Sprinkle candy confetti over frosting. Make windows in center of largest disk with orange Life-Savers. Base of cake may be pizza cardboard disk covered with foil.

U.F.O. Cake

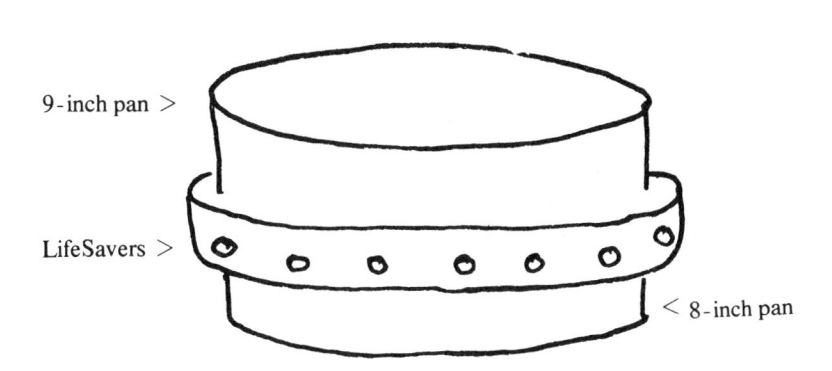

9-inch pan >

LifeSavers >

< 8-inch pan

Activities:

Arrival — Color tablecloth and make costumes.

Space Wars March — After children have created costumes, put them on and march around the room. For effect, darken room and play theme music from space movies. Lighting may be from laser beam flashlights.

Alpha Omega Commands — Children pretend to be new robots which must be inspected for efficiency in following commands. As Alpha Omega gives directions, children in robotlike movements obey commands only if they are preceded by "Alpha Omega says. . . ." Any robots who move without the name clue need to go back to the factory.

Space Tunnels — Build a space tunnel as illustrated using cardboard tubes glued to a base. Give each child four marbles. Children take turns rolling the marbles into tunnels from about three feet away.

Space Tunnel

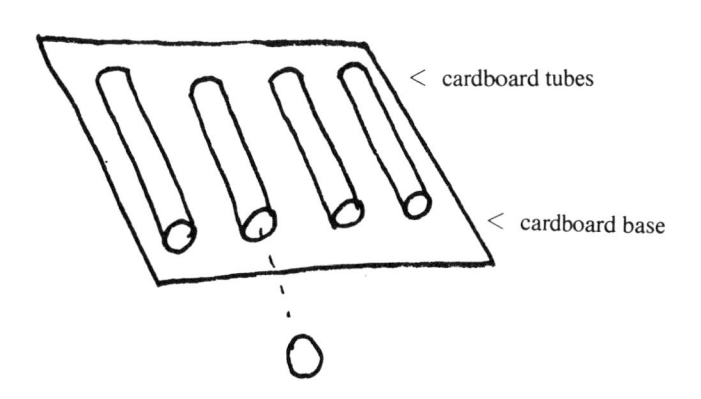

< cardboard tubes

< cardboard base

Favors:

Space Dust — Presweetened fruit drink packaged in small pregummed envelopes.
Star Stickers
Space Puppets
Space Comic Books

Community Helpers Birthday Rally

Community Helpers Birthday Rally

Ages: 3-6 years

Invitations:

Cut a double figure of a person. Creatively decorate front to resemble a community helper (such as a fireman or doctor). Place message on inside fold.

Decorations:

Room — Pictures, dolls, and articles associated with different types of community helpers.

Community Village — Collect large cartons from a grocery or appliance store. Cut out a door in each carton so children can crawl in and make windows so they can peek out. Using magic markers, tempera paint mixed with liquid starch, or construction paper, decorate the cartons to represent community buildings such as a fire station, police station, school or post office.

Menu and Recipes:

Teacher's Crackers — Break graham crackers into sections. Put letters on each with squirt-on cheese spread. Before eating the crackers children spell words or identify letters.

Fireman's Punch — Use a favorite red punch.

Fire Hoses — Spread ham and bologna slices with cottage or cream cheese, then roll up.

Community Helpers Sheet Cake — Bake favorite recipe for sheet cake. Frost, then decorate to look like a fire station, police car, school, or community helper.

Activities:

Pretend — Assemble clothing and props to be used for community helpers dramatic play. Children dress up in costumes of community helpers and use props and community village boxes for play. Encourage discussion about how community workers assist others.

Do You Know? (Sing song to the tune of "Muffin Man"):

"Do you know the policeman, the policeman, the policeman?
Do you know the policeman? He protects us."

Make up verses for doctor, nurse, teacher, etc.

(Last verse tells what helper does) — Ex.: The doctor makes us well.
The nurse helps the doctor.
The teacher helps us learn.

Who Am I? — Place pictures of community helpers in a box. A child picks out a card, then acts the role of that community helper. The other children try to guess who he is portraying. The child who guesses correctly gets to have next turn to choose a card.

Heavy Traffic — Use props for policeman, such as hat, badge, and white gloves. Choose one child to be the policeman. The other children stand at a base line about twenty feet away from him. The policeman turns his back to children and counts from 1 to 10, either fast or slow. He then says "Heavy Traffic" and turns quickly around. The children who are running toward him freeze as he turns. If he calls the names of those still moving they must return to base line. The policeman then turns and counts again. The first child to reach the policeman or goal line gets to be the next policeman.

Pin the Badge on the Policeman — Make a large picture of a policeman minus his badge. Using a paper badge play a variation of "Pin the Tail on the Donkey."

Ring the Fire Bell — Assemble a bell, Nerf balls, or bean bags. Hang the bell in doorway or from a rafter. Children try to hit the bell by throwing balls or bean bags. Award a point for each hit.

Guess My Job — Assign a name of a community helper to each child. The child who is chosen to be "It" is blindfolded. Other children run near "It." If caught, a clue must be given which will help "It" guess who they represent. If he guesses correctly the child caught takes his place. If he cannot guess the child is freed.

< Policeman

< Badge

Pin the Badge on the Policeman

Doctor

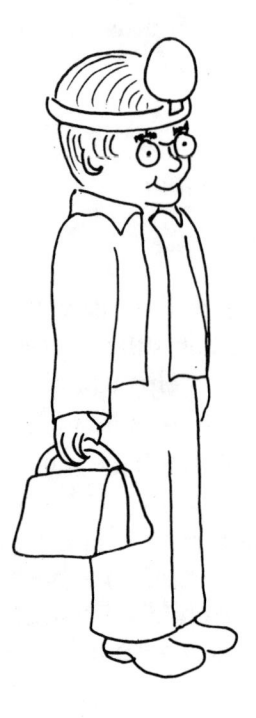

Nurse

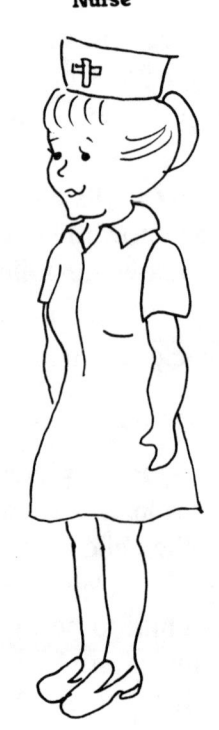

C. B. Truckers Birthday Rally

Breaker, Breaker...
Hey all you CBers, got your ears on?
Put the petal to the metal
and join the birthday convoy
for an eyeballing at Terry's home
– M twenty, May 16 — 1400 hours

10-4 Good Buddy....

C. B. Truckers Birthday Rally

Ages: 8-12 years

Invitations:

Front of invitation can be a truck with a driver talking on a CB. The message invitation should be written in CB language. (Example: Cruise your wheels to Jim's garage.)

Decorations:

Room — Pictures of trucks, signs with CB comments, etc. around the room.

"Keep on Truckin" Table — Cover table with plain white tablecloth. Arrange crepe paper strips to resemble roads. Along the roads place models of cars and trucks. Use straws, paper scraps, and clay bases to create miniature road signs. Place in center of table the CB cake. Decorate paper plates to represent a steering wheel. Fold colored napkins into a rectangle, then add wheels and windows with construction paper circles and squares.

Menu and Recipes:

Chili and Crackers
Assorted Vegetables
Milk

On the Road Cake — Two layer devil's food cake with chocolate icing. Use cake decorator to make lines representing roads. Complete with road signs represented by red and green gum drops stuck on toothpick. Make miniature cars as described below.

Miniature Cars for CB Truckers — Make miniature cars out of orange-colored, peanut-shaped candy. Cut a wedge out of top for seat. Attach M&Ms for wheels and spare tire on back. Outline seat and bumper with flute frosting. Make headlights with a dot of icing.

Activities:

Breaker Breaker — Present each child with a CB vocabulary sheet. Ask each child to write a message using CB codes.

Lost Cargo — Divide children into groups. Give each group a coded CB message which, if followed, will lead to hidden treasure. Treasure boxes could include prizes such as comics, small cars, or candy.

Spin a Yarn — Children sit in a circle. The birthday child holds a ball of yarn and starts a story about a cross-country journey. When the timer goes off, he throws the ball of yarn to someone else, but holds onto the end of the string. The child catching the yarn continues the story and when timer goes off, holds onto string and throws ball of yarn to someone else. Continue until both yarn and story are in a tangle.

CB Secret — Children divide into small groups of three or four. Give each group a secret CB message, which they are to decode. When time is called each group will share with other the message they unscrambled.

Fat Load Relay — Divide players into two teams. Provide each team with a wagon filled with toys, etc. Explain that the teams are two trucking companies who are trying to prove they can move cargo faster than any other team. At the "go" signal the leader if each team pulls wagon to a certain point, then back where another "driver" takes over. If any of the items fall out of the wagon, the driver must stop, pick them up and then return to the starting line to begin again. First team to finish wins.

"Breaker Breaker" — (A Simple Simon variation)
Play as Simple Simon except that clue words are "Breaker Breaker." State directions such as "Breaker Breaker, back your truck four steps" or "Breaker, Breaker, run them engines right in place!"

CB Lingo

Affirmative — yes
Anchor it — stop
Bear — police
Back off — slow down
Bear trap — speed trap
Bring it on — please reply
Bubble Gum Machine — police car w/ flashing light
Buffalo — man
Camera — police radar
Casa — home
Coffee pot — restaurant
Coke stop — restroom break
Come on — your turn to talk
DDT — warning; don't do that
Drop the hammer — speed up
Doughnut — tire
Double nickel — 55 m.p.h.

Double seven — negative; no
Ears — CB set
Evel Knievel — motorcycle rider
Flop it — turn around
Kiddie Car — school bus
M-20 — location; meeting place
Negative — no
Rat Race — heavy traffic
Read — understand; hear
Roger — yes, also 10-4
Rubber Duck — lead vehicle in a CB convoy
Shoot an eyeball — take a look
Side door — passing lane
Skating rink — slippery road
Tailgate — follow too closely
Z's — sleep

Old MacDonald's Barnyard Birthday Fling

Old MacDonald's Barnyard Birthday Fling

Ages: 3-6 years

Invitations:

Haystack shape cut out of yellow construction paper with Old MacDonald resting on haystack.

Decorations:

Door — Draw around child on large wrapping paper. Decorate the features to represent Old MacDonald.

Room — Hay, cornstalks, scarecrow, maize, and pictures or models of farm scenes.

Table — Checkered tablecloth. In front of each plate have an animal place card. Use the farm birthday cake as the centerpiece.

Menu and Recipes:

Piggies in the Poke — Slice unsliced loaf of bread lengthwise. Cut in half. Spread with ketchup. Roll around hot dog. Cut into bite-sized pieces.

Hen's Eggs — Hard boiled eggs.

Old MacDonald's Garden — Use carrot, celery, cucumber, and green pepper sticks. Place in a 13-by-11-inch pan. Cover with strips of brown paper which are crisscrossed like a lattice. Children use toothpicks to "dig" a vegetable out of the garden.

Strawberry Moo — Add approximately 1 teaspoon strawberry jelly to 1 cup of milk. Mix in blender.

Barnyard Fling Cake — Bake favorite chocolate sheet cake. Cover with chocolate frosting. Place animal crackers around rim of cake. Complete farm scene with a miniature barn, fence, and tractor.

Activities:

Arrival — (1) Children may build a farm with boxes, blocks, and toy animals. (2) Have paper and crayons so pictures of a farm can be created. (3) Place books about farms around the room. (4) Sing and play "Old MacDonald Had a Farm" or "The Farmer in the Dell."

Animal Hunt — Before the party hide small plastic animals around party area. At "go" signal, children hunt for animals. They may keep those found. Hint: Have a few extra for those children who did not find an animal.

Animal Fair — Provide play dough and animal-shaped cookie cutters. Children may roll, punch, and shape clay. After an animal form has been sculptured add buttons, sequins, or cloth scraps for features. Place in a box that represents a barn.

Barnyard — Invite children to pretend to be an animal by moving and making appropriate sounds. The activity can be initiated by showing animal pictures or talking about animals that live on a farm.

Duck, Duck, Goose — Children sit in circle. The child who is "It" touches others softly on the head and says "Duck." When the word "Goose" is substituted the child tagged tries to catch "It" before he completes the run around the circle and sits down in the vacated spot. If the tagged child does not catch "It" he exchanges roles in the game.

Tortoise and Hare — Place a goal several feet from the start line. The leader "Hare" runs around children who are standing at the start line. When he taps the shoulder of another child both race toward the finish goal. The player who reaches the goal first is the winner and leader for the next time.

Old MacDonald Feeds His Animals — Children sit in a circle. The first child starts the game by naming one animal fed by Old MacDonald. "Old MacDonald feeds a horse on his farm." The next child repeats the first sentence, then adds another animal. "Old MacDonald feeds a horse and a lamb on his farm." Continue with each child adding another animal.

Barnyard Friends

Pirate Birthday Bash

Pirate Birthday Bash

Ages: 5-8 years

Invitations:

Use either the pirate illustration on the preceding page or make a construction paper treasure chest and write messages inside.

Decorations:

Pirate Puppet

Room — Pirate puppets, Jolly Roger flags (see illustration), pirate ships, a pirate dummy made by stuffing a pillow case or a large bag for the head and putting old clothes over a broomstick. Remember to put a patch over one eye. The end of the broomstick can be used as a peg leg. Drop dummy in the corner of the room.

Centerpiece — Paint a shoe box and lid black. Attach the lid to the box and fill it with shredded newspaper. Cover shredded newspaper with a sheet of metallic paper. Add a layer of gold-wrapped chocolate coins and pieces of jewelry.

Place Mats — Skull and Crossbones: Cut a skull and crossbones out of white construction paper and add features using a black magic marker. Glue to a black construction paper oval.

Place Cards — Cut a double eye patch out of black construction paper. Write child's name on it using a white crayon or grease pencil. Next punch out two holes near the fold and thread a piece of black yarn through the holes. Children can wear later as part of their costumes.

Menu and Recipes:

Plankwiches — Trim the crust off of bread slices and cut them into thirds. Spread pieces with a favorite filling and top with another piece of bread.

Banana/Pineapple Treasures — Peel and slice 6 large bananas and add 1 can of unsweetened pineapple. Chill. Pour off juice just before serving.

Pieces o' Eight — Peel and thinly slice sweet potatoes. Fry them in a pan of deep oil. Drain on paper towels and lightly sprinkle with either salt or sugar.

Pirate's Brew
---
1 gallon apple juice ⅔ 46-oz. can pineapple juice
⅔ of 6-oz. can frozen orange juice juice of 2 lemons
cloves to taste ¾ box cinnamon sticks

Combine all ingredients in a saucepan. Simmer for 30 minutes. Pour into punch bowl. Garnish with sliced oranges.

Treasure Map Cake — Frost cake with a white or light blue tinted frosting. Soften black licorice strings by placing in a warm oven for 2 or 3 minutes. Place them in sandblown patterns over the cake. Next add landmarks such as water, forests, mountains, and sand using appropriate colored frosting.

Arrival:

Pirate Costumes — Each guest makes a pirate hat, an eye patch, buckles for his shoes, etc.

Marionettes — Pre-cut body pieces out of large pieces of poster board and punch holes as directed (see illustrations). Put one marionette together so the children can use it as a guide when selecting pieces for their marionettes. Provide magic markers, fabric, yarn scraps, etc., for the children to use in decorating their creation. Hang and display the puppets and allow the children to take them home after the party.

Walk the Plank — Place a 2-inch-by-2-inch-by-8-foot board on the floor. Make at least eight to ten cards with a simple balance stunt on each (for younger children, you might want to draw an illustration of the stunt.) Examples of stunts are: walk across beam carrying a bean bag on your head; walk across beam with your eyes closed; walk across beam while tossing a bean bag in the air; walk to center of beam, turn around once, continue to walk to the end; walk across beam with giant steps; walk across beam, stop at center, and throw a bean bag into a box; walk sideways, left foot leading; walk across beam with baby steps, etc.

Children line up in front of the plank. The first child picks a card. Each child has a turn to follow the instructions on the card while walking the plank. Any child who steps off the beam has to stay in the "water" until another child steps off the beam to replace him. Continue to play until each child has had an opportunity to pick a card or they tire of the game.

Cannon Ball Volley — Use two long ropes to define two 6-foot areas that are "ships." Put the ropes about 8 feet apart. Provide approximately eight Nerf or yarn balls. Players are divided into two equal teams and each team is given four balls. On the signal "go" they throw their balls into the other ship. The game continues for approximately two minutes. When the leader calls "Freeze" all throwing stops. The balls are counted and the team with the least number of balls wins.

Treasure Hunt (for younger children) — Dye two to three boxes of toothpicks using food coloring. Toss them in the yard. Allow children five minutes to find as many toothpicks as possible. Provide prizes.

Treasure Ships — Give each child a piece of aluminum foil. Fold to create a boat. When the boats are complete float them in a pan of water. Designate paper clips as "treasures." Add paper clips, one at a time, to determine the boat that can carry the greatest treasure without sinking.

Pirate and the Prisoner — Divide the group into two teams. One team is called pirates; the other team is called the prisoners. Define an area (called the ship) for the captured prisoners. At the signal, the pirates try to tag as many prisoners as they can and take them to the ship. Prisoners must stay in the ship until they are touched by another prisoner. At the end of five minutes, free all prisoners, have the children switch roles, and play the game again.

Treasures to Remember — Place twelve to fifteen treasures like bracelets, rings, hair bands, necklaces, etc., on a tray. Cover with a cloth. To play, remove cloth and invite children to study tray carefully for about one minute. Cover again. See how many items children can remember seeing. Perhaps each child can then choose "a treasure" as a favor.

Jellybean Treasures — Before party make twenty clue cards and fill twenty small plastic bags with one to twenty jellybeans. To each bag attach a tag that identifies the number of jellybeans inside. Hide the bags around party area. At party, divide group into teams of four or five players. Pass out an equal number of clue cards to each team. In a time limit of three minutes see how many treasures can be found.

Clue Cards

1 – solo
2 – duet
3 – number in Billy Goat Gruff family
4 – two pairs
5 – fingers on one hand
6 – half a dozen
7 – number of dwarfs who like Snow White
8 – number of feet of an octopus
9 – one less than ten.
10 – feet of five children
11 – number on a football team who can play on field
12 – noon
13 – a baker's dozen
14 – a dozen plus two
15 – three nickels
16 – ounces in a pound
17 – three nickels and two pennies
18 – three times six
19 – one less than twenty
20 – price of a stamp

Birthday Record Hop

< put two dancers on top

< dark icing "grooves"

Oreo cookie cutter >

white icing >

< dark mints with icing for "notes"

Birthday Record Hop

Ages: 9-15 years

Invitations:
Record disk made with white lines drawn on black paper. Inside message asks guests to bring favorite records.

Decorations:
Posters of pop artists, mobiles of instruments and albums and record covers placed around room. Arrange room with large area for dancing.

Menu and Recipes:

Do It Yourself Sandwiches — Set out a variety of breads, meats, cheeses, and spreads.

Potato Chips and Sour Cream Dip — Make by blending sour cream with dry onion soup mix.

Vegetable Tray with Dip — Assorted fresh vegetables with dip made by mixing in blender, then chilling:

8 oz. tomato sauce	8 oz. cream cheese
6 slices crisp bacon, drained and crumbled	¼ teaspoon instant onion
2 drops of hot pepper sauce	

Party Mix

½ cup butter	1 cup salad oil
2 tablespoons Worcestershire sauce	1 teaspoon Tabasco sauce
garlic and celery salt to taste	1 box of Cheerios
1 box of Rice Chex	1 box of Pretzel sticks
½ lb. mixed salted nuts	

Blend together, bake for 1½ hours at 200°, stirring occasionally.

Choice of Soft Drinks

Dancin' Cake — Use favorite chocolate cake recipe. Bake in two layers. Use a white icing as frosting. Tint part of the icing a dark color to make rings to represent a record. Center disk and musical notes are made with mint or oreo cookies. Place boy and girl figurines on cake.

Cake Figurines

Activities:

String Maze — Have as many strings as children invited to party. Before the party place in game room. Strings can criss-cross and go around or over and under furniture. When party starts each guest selects a string and starts winding it around a pencil until he finds his prize.

That's My Name — Ask each guest to write his name on three strips of paper. Place all names in a bag. In a central area place five or six prizes. Start pulling names out of the bag. Each time a guest hears his name he selects a prize from the pile or takes one from another guest. Prizes pass back and forth between participants as names are pulled. Those still holding a prize when all names have been called win.

Name That Tune — Before the party, record on tape theme segments of ten popular tunes. At party give each player or team a pencil and paper. Ask guests to listen carefully to a few bars of each song. Then write on paper the name of song and performer. Award five points for each correct title name and a bonus as artist or band is recognized. Replay the tape as answers are checked. Award prizes.

Record Scramble — Scramble the names of about ten popular hit records. Make duplicate copies, enough for each player or team. At the "go" signal players try to unscramble as many themes as possible in time allocated.

Dancin' to the Beat — Invite each guest to choose a favorite song for others to hear from his album. Arrange for an older teenager to come to the party and teach single dance routines that do not necessarily require boy-girl partners.

Under the Broom — Place a broom bridge over two stacks of books approximately 16 inches high. After each player has a turn crawling under the bridge, remove a book from each stack. If a player touches when crawling under the broom he is out. The one who crawls through the lowest space is the winner.

4
Birthdays Around the World

Leprechaun Hideaway Birthday

Leprechaun Hideaway Birthday

Ages: 5-10 years

Invitations:
Picture of leprechaun on toadstool with rainbow and pot of gold. Room decorated with leprechauns, mushrooms, and crepe paper rainbows.

Decorations:
Green tablecloth

Mushrooms — made with small nut cups draped over paper cylinders.

Shamrocks — for decorating placecards and napkins.

Centerpiece — made by stacking rounded stones on tray. Place leprechaun on stones. Add pots of gold with candy coins and mushroom nut cups.

Menu and Recipes:
Ham Roll Ups — Roll thin ham

Irish Spuds — Small baked potatoes

Rainbow Salad
1 can #2 fruit cocktail   4 packages of Jello (lemon, lime, strawberry, and orange)
1 cup whipped cream   1 cup miniature marshmallows

Congeal lime, strawberry, and orange Jello in separate pans. Drain one #2 can fruit cocktail – reserve syrup. Add enough water to syrup to make 1½ cups liquid. Heat to boiling and pour over one package of lemon Jello. Chill until syrupy, then whip until frothy. Fold in fruit cocktail, 1 cup whipped cream and 1 cup miniature marshmallows. Cut congealed Jello in cubes. Fold into lemon Jello mixture. Pour into molds. Chill until congealed.

St. Patrick's Day Cake — Make a two-layer cake from mix. Frost with marshmallow or snowpeak frosting. To make shamrocks slice green gumdrops, then arrange in groupings of three. Draw a stem for each shamrock. Arrange green mint leaves around base of cake plate.

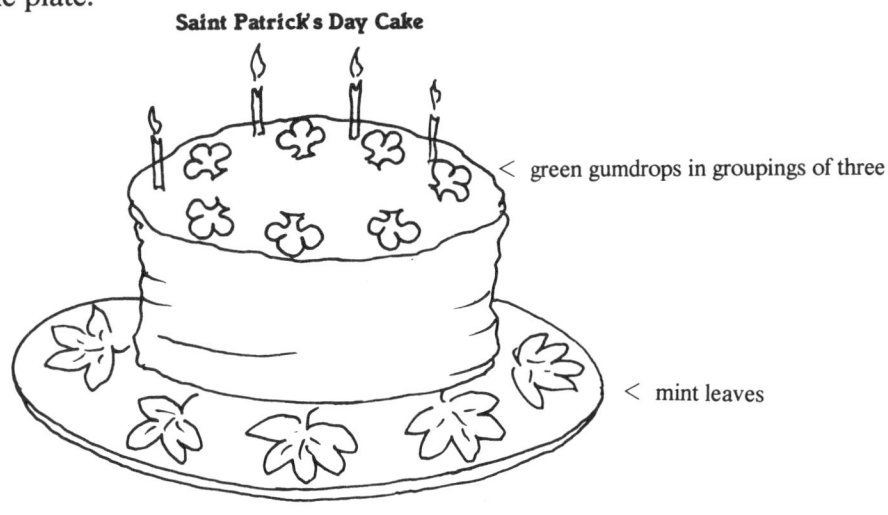

Saint Patrick's Day Cake

< green gumdrops in groupings of three

< mint leaves

Irish Mist — Add lime sherbet to ginger ale. In each glass place a striped straw that is decorated with a marshmallow.

Activities:

Wearin' of the Green — Invite each child to wear something green to the party. Make a cloak by using a semi-circle of green crepe paper. A tall cap can be made by stapling a half circle of green construction paper into a cone shape.

Leprechaun Steal — Children sit in semi-circle. One child pretends to be the leprechaun asleep a few feet in front of others. Placed behind him is the treasure, a small pot filled with gold coin candies. Point to a child who will tiptoe quietly up to the leprechaun, steal the pot, and then hide it behind him. After the leprechaun awakens he has two guesses in which to identify who snatched the pot. If he doesn't guess the name of the thief, the child who stole the pot gets to keep it. If the leprechaun guesses, that child becomes the next leprechaun.

Shamrock Hunt — Prior to party make three shamrocks per child. Hide around the party area. At the "go" signal children hunt for shamrocks. The child with most shamrocks wins a prize.

Shamrock

Leprechaun Reflections — Divide the guests into two groups and give each member of one group a green cone hat made out of construction paper to wear. Then ask the children in the other group to pretend that they are mirrors. Tell them that each child should pick a Leprechaun (a child wearing a green hat) and reflect his movements. If the Leprechaun puts his left arm out, then his partner must put his right arm out. The adult should make a few body movements and ask the children to reflect them to help them better understand the aspects of mirroring before they divide up into pairs. After approximately 5 minutes, children should switch roles. Prizes could be awarded to the pair who make the funniest, best, worst, happiest, saddest, etc. reflection.

Jolly Old England Birthday Celebration

Jolly Old England Birthday Celebration

Ages: 5-9 years

Invitations:

A picture of a jester in front of folded construction paper. Write message in Old English form:

> Hear ye, Hear ye,
> Come to the Wilson Castle
> Bells at 15 hours, Thursday, the Twelfth day of May
> Celebrate the 6th Birthday of Master Jack.

Decorations:

Castle — Stack boxes or blocks to make a castle. Use cardboard cylinders for towers. Top towers with cones of construction paper.

Maypole — Attach rainbow colors of crepe paper or ribbons to a pole (a carpet tubeboard could be an excellent pole).

Table — Use a checkered tablecloth and pewter type dishes.

Place Cards — Cone hats with Old English names such as Friar John, Sir Randy, Lady Jane, or Gallant William.

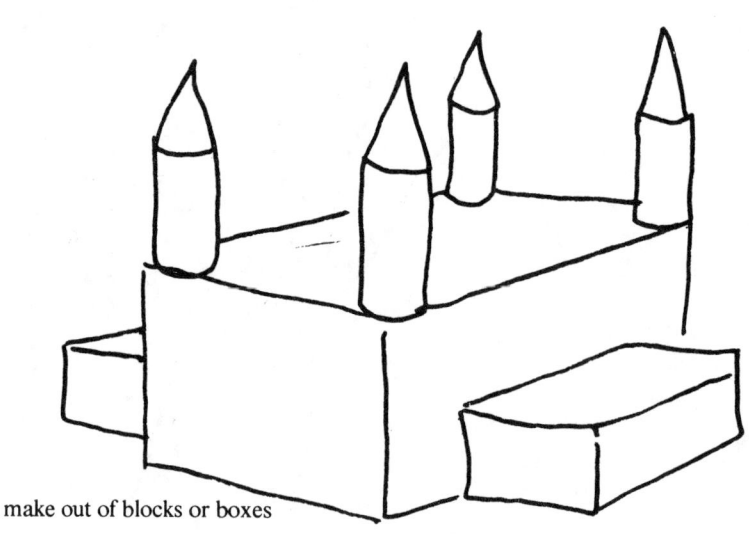

Napkins — Place a paper jester on the corner of each napkin.

Boy's Clothing — Robin Hood could be a green crepe paper cloak and cone hat made with construction paper.

Old English Castle

make out of blocks or boxes

Cone Hats

< half circles

< fold and staple

< streamers

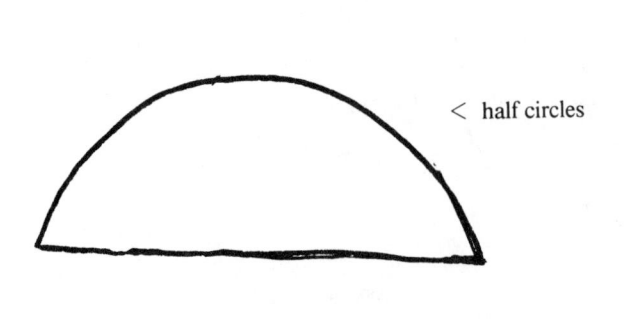

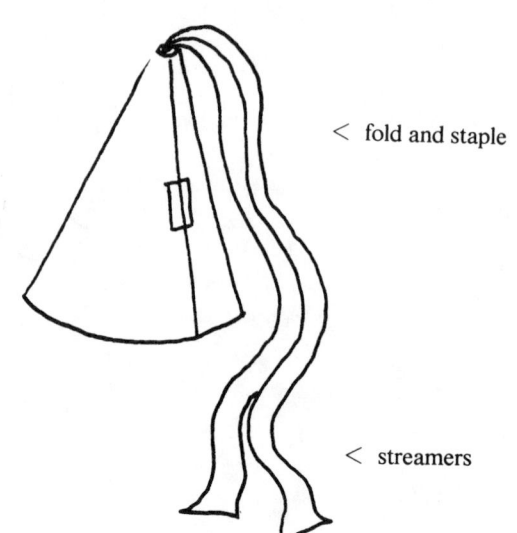

Girl's Clothing— Lady Marion Garb— A construction paper cone hat decorated with ribbons and ties or cap made with a circle of cloth with elastic sewn around edge. Girls may also enjoy wearing their long dresses or skirts.

Menu and Recipes:

Checkerboard Sandwiches— Use brown and white bread. Arrange sandwiches in checkerboard fashion on a large tray.

Jester Salad— Cut a banana in half lengthwise. Place on lettuce. Decorate with a pineapple ring, maraschino cherries, raisins, and marshmallows.

Royal Coconut Cake— Bake favorite coconut cake in three layers. Frost with a 7-minute frosting. Place coconut on top. If available, add a figurine of a queen or king.

Robin Hood Punch— A favorite green punch.

Activities:

Arrival— Make costumes

Robin Hood Obstacles— Explain that the Merry Men of Sherwood Forest had to be skilled and agile. Members had to prove they could jump rivers, leap over castle walls, crawl through tunnels and keep balance while walking on fences. Children then try their skills on the following obstacles. Encourage them to repeat activities to increase skills.

>*Jumping Rivers*– Place two ropes about two feet apart. Children jump trying to get across both ropes. Lengthen the distance between ropes until it is too wide for most to jump.
>
>*Leap the Castle Wall*– Hold a 12-foot rope on both ends. Start with the rope about a foot off the ground. After each child leaps over it raise it a few more inches. Continue until it is too high for most.
>
>*Crawling through tunnels*– Hold rope on both ends at about knee level. Children take turns crawling under. Continue to lower rope until it is too low for any to crawl under.
>
>*Balancing on Fences*– Stretch rope on ground. Children walk from end to end without falling off. If a balance beam or low stone wall is available use that instead.

Jester Tricks— Provide a paper crown for one child who pretends to be the unhappy king or queen. Explain that jesters try to make the king and queen happy by doing funny tricks. The children then take turns doing funny jester tricks. The one who brings a smile to the face of the king or queen becomes the monarch for the next turn.

Drop the Handkerchief— Provide a handkerchief or cloth square. Children form a circle. The child who is "It" runs behind others and drops the handkerchief behind a child. The child picks up the handkerchief then chases "It" around the circle. If he does not catch him before "It" reaches a vacant spot, places are exchanged.

Hot Potato— Provide a ball or bean bag and a noise maker. Children sit in a circle. Tell them to pretend that the ball is a potato that is too hot to handle. They then rapidly pass it around the circle, trying not to have it at the sound of the noise maker.

Skittles— Provide ten plastic ½-gallon milk containers or plastic bowling pins, a ball, and a backdrop board. Place the pins in bowling formation. Players stand approximately ten feet away from the pins. Keep score. Give one point for each pin knocked over. The first child to win 50 points wins the game.

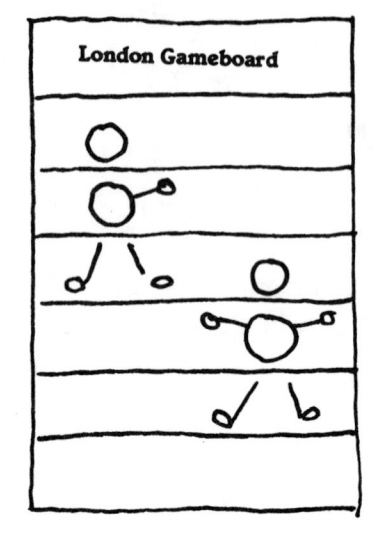

London — Mark sidewalk with chalk as illustrated. Divide players into two teams. When players take their turn they stand about 5 feet behind base line. The first player of one team throws a disk and draws a head on the space where it lands. The leader of the second team does the same. The next players throw disk, trying to reach a proper space for the body. Again, draw the form where the disk lands. Continue the game until the forms of two men are completed. If the disk lands on the space called London or outside the side boundary lines no body part can be drawn. The drawings will probably be strange and bring a lot of laughter.

Noble Duke of York — Chant or sing and while doing so, follow directions of the song. Children march forward, backward, stand up, squat down, and stand halfway up.

"Oh, the Noble Duke of York
He had ten thousand men.
He marched them up to the top of the hill,
Then he marched them back again.
And when you're up, you're up.
And when you're down, you're down.
And when you're only halfway up,
You're neither up nor down.

Animal Safari Birthday Party

< animal crackers

< M & Ms

< greenery

Jungle Friends

Animal Safari Birthday Party

Ages: 4-7 years

Invitations:

Animal pictures created by the birthday child; colorfully decorated and placed on front fold of invitation.

Decorations:

Animal Faces — Select a variety of sizes of paper plates. Large plates can remain in original shape or have a cone effect by cutting out a wedge from rim to center, then stapling sides together. Smaller plates or nut cups can be used to represent nose and ears. Have cotton balls, bits of fur, felt, and pipe cleaners available for adding features. If faces are to be used as a mask, cut out holes for eyes. Fasten a string to each side. Tie strings behind the head.

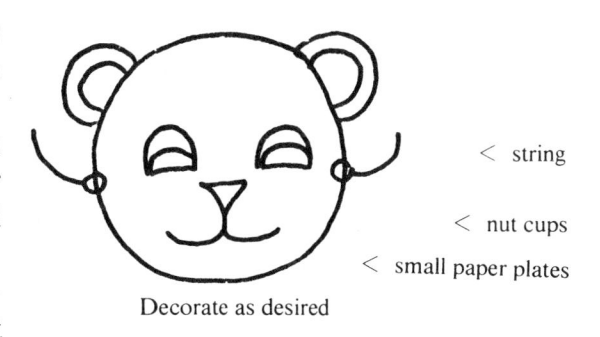

Animal Faces

< string
< nut cups
< small paper plates

Decorate as desired

Animal Mobiles — Cut construction paper into strips of various widths and lengths. Children paste rings together to form shapes of animals. Have bits of paper scraps and markers so that features can be added. Hang from rafters or light fixtures.

Animal Mobile

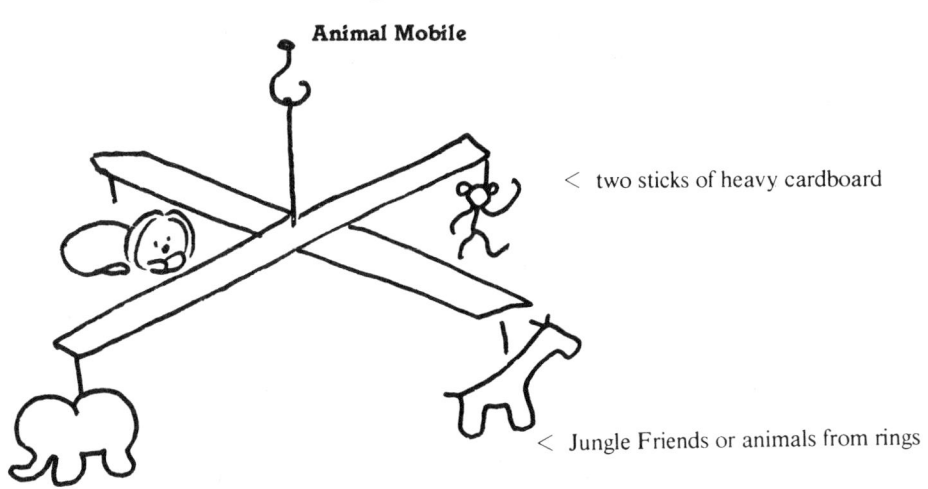

< two sticks of heavy cardboard
< Jungle Friends or animals from rings

Table — Use a fabric table cloth with a pattern that represents an animal coat. Napkin rings can be 3-inch cardboard strips colored in an animal coat pattern, then stapled at ends.

Animal Place Cards — Make finger puppets with semicircles of construction paper. Add a triangle, round, oval, or square shape for head. Decorate with magic markers. Tape a name strip at the base with the child's name plus that of the animal. (Terry Tiger, Molly Monkey, or Ellen Elephant).

Menu and Recipes:

Jungle Pancakes — Favorite pancake recipe mixed a little thinner than usual. Drop on grill and form funny animal shapes.

Monkey's Delight — Nut cups filled with peanuts, cereals, and raisins.

Banana Zoo — Create a funny animal with a banana. Use toothpicks with marshmallows or gumdrops for legs, feet, and facial features. (Other fruits and vegetables can be decorated in the same way).

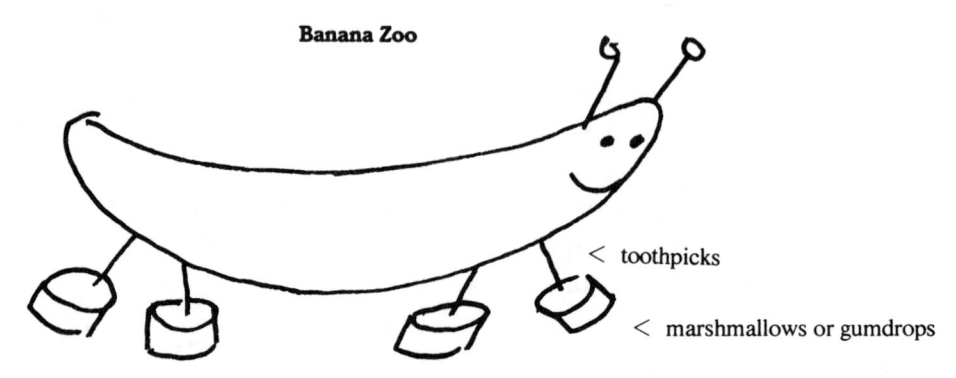

Banana Zoo

< toothpicks

< marshmallows or gumdrops

Tiger Punch — Orange or tangerine juice.

Animal Parade Birthday Cake — Bake favorite devil's food cake mix in two layer pans. Cover with chocolate frosting. Place animal crackers in ring around edge. Decorate between crackers with M & Ms to represent footprints. Place candles in center.

OR

Animal Ice Cream Parade — Cut ice cream into square slices about 2 inches thick. Place between two graham crackers, then onto a small saucer or paper plate. Stick animal crackers on each bar of ice cream. Set all plates in center of table. Add a toy train engine that appears to be pulling the cars with jungle animals.

Activities:

Animal Parade — Children use animal masks and march around the room to a record such as "Carnival of Animals."

Swim, Fly, or Run — Have all children find a space of their own (a distance away from another child). At the suggestion of an animal action, such as, "whales swim," all children respond by making a swimming motion. When suggestions are incorrect ("Hippos fly"), children do not move.

Jungle Lotto — Collect duplicate sets of animal pictures from magazines, inexpensive picture dictionaries or nature stamps. Paste animal pictures in groups of six onto cards. Make enough cards so that there will be one for each guest. Place the duplicate picture of each animal in a box. To play the game each player selects a lotto card. As a picture is drawn from the box the child who has the duplicate says, "I have the giraffe," then places the picture on the lotto card. The first child to completely cover animals on his card wins. For a variation to use with older children, use the same lotto cards but instead of duplicate pictures write clues that will identify the animal.

Find My Baby — Collect pictures of animal mothers and babies from magazines, newspapers, inexpensive books, or stamps. Before the party hide pictures of babies around the room. At the start of game give each child a picture of a mother animal. Explain that the mother needs help in finding her baby. At signal, the child searches for the correct baby.

Find My Tail — Draw or collect pictures of animals; then cut off tails. Children play the game by attaching tails on the correct animals.

Pin the Tail on the Monkey — Draw a picture of a monkey minus a tail. Make a tail out of heavy yarn or construction paper. Play the same way as "Pin the Tail on the Donkey."

Lion Chase — A chant in which directions and motions of leader are repeated by group.

"Let's go on a lion hunt....OK?"
    (nod head)
"We'll walk down the path....OK?"
    (tap hands on knees)
"Oh, oh. Tall grass. Gotta go through it....OK?"
    (make arm motions to represent pushing back tall grass)
"Oh, oh. Short grass. Gotta go through it....OK?"
    (make arm motions to represent sweeping back short grass)
"Let's walk on....OK?"
    (tap hands on knees)
"Oh, oh. Tall tree....Gotta climb it....OK?"
    (make climbing motion with hands)
"Look around....Let's go higher....OK?"
    (circle eyes then climb again)
"Let's slide down fast....OK?"
    (bring hands down in sliding motion)
"Oh, oh. Here's a big river....Gotta swim it....OK?"
    (make swimming motions)
"That was fun. Let's do it again....OK?"
    (swimming motion again)
"Oh, oh. On the wrong side....Gotta do it again....OK?"
    (swimming motion)
"Let's move on....OK?"
    (tap knees)
"Oh, oh. There's the lion's cave....Gotta go in....OK?"
    (tap fingers very lightly on knees)
"Oooooooo, it's very dark in here!"
    (put finger rings to eyes)
"Gotta move on....OK?"
    (tap fingers lightly)
"Let's look around....OK?"
    (finger rings to eyes)
"Oh, oh. There's the lion....Gotta run home....OK?"
    (repeat all movements in reverse)
"We're home....but we didn't catch the lion! Phew!"
    (wipe forehead in relief)

Save the Monkey — One child pretends to be a hungry tiger and another, a little monkey. Children stand in a circle and hold hands. Place the tiger outside of the circle and the monkey inside. At signal, "go," the tiger tries to catch the monkey by getting in or out of the arm bridges. The children try to protect the monkey by raising and lowering arms to keep tiger out. When monkey is caught choose new players to be the tiger and monkey.

Pizza Birthday Festival

Lou
is gonna be 8.
Come on Saturday
at 11:30
To help make the pizza,
Eat some food,
And play some games.

Pizza Birthday Festival

Ages: 6-10 years

Invitations:
A pizza circle. Write message on inside cover in broken Italian dialect.

Decorations:
Red checkered cloth, flags, maps, and travel posters of Italy. Have paper and paints available so young artists can create a masterpiece to hang.

Menu and Recipes:
Pizza — Use favorite dough recipe. Divide dough so that each child can make his own pizza. Have a variety of meats and cheeses so pizzas can be made to suit taste.

Vegetable Sticks — Celery, carrots, green pepper, squash, etc.

Pistachio Ice Cream

Leaning Tower of Pisa Cookies — Make sugar cookies in tilted rectangle shape.

Activities:
Leaning Tower of Pisa — Take blocks and stack them one at a time a little off center. See who can build the tallest building.

Italian Folk Games

Nut Throw — Use English walnuts, filberts, or other nuts to make about ten castles (three nuts stacked). Set castles several inches apart. Each child gets ten nuts to throw. See who can knock down the most castles.

Bimbo or *Luck Leaf* — One player is chosen to be the Bimbo. He is given two small leaves. Others form two lines, each facing the other about 15 feet apart. Each child keeps his hands behind him with palms open. The Bimbo walks slowly up and down behind the two lines and quietly drops a leaf in one child's hand in each line. After dropping the second leaf, he walks on, then suddenly calls, "Stop! Thief! Lucky Leaf." The two players who have leaves run as fast as possible to the other line. When they reach the line, each tries to drop leaf in hands of another player. That player, in turn, passes the leaf to the next in line because no player wants the Bimbo to catch him holding the leaf. When the player is caught with leaf in hand, he becomes the next Bimbo and the game starts again.

Wolf and Lamb — Children form circle and hold hands. A wolf is chosen and stands on the outside of the circle. A lamb cries, "I am a lamb." The wolf then says, "I am a wolf and I'll catch you." The lamb states, "Oh, no, you won't." The wolf tries to get inside the circle to catch the lamb, but the children in circle try to keep him out. If he succeeds in breaking into the circle, the children help the lamb by letting him outside, then trying to keep the wolf inside. If the lamb is caught, he joins the circle. The wolf chooses a new wolf and he becomes the lamb.

Follow Chase — Players make a circle and stretch arms to put hands on neighbor's shoulders. On opposite sides of circle stand a "runner" and a "chaser." The chaser tries to catch the runner but he must take the same route as the runner. When the runner is caught, he must join the circle. The chaser chooses a replacement and game starts again.

Italian Nine Pins — Set the pins up as illustrated. (Chalk or masking tape can be used to identify position for each plastic pin or milk carton filled with sand). Identify a line for bowlers to stand behind. Take turns bowling with a medium-sized rubber ball. Each player scores a point for each pin knocked down. After bowling each player runs forward and replaces fallen pins to upright position, then runs back to give the ball to the next child in line. Continue until all have had a turn to bowl a set number of times.

Italian Nine Pins

Milk cartons filled with sand >
or
Plastic pins bought from the store >

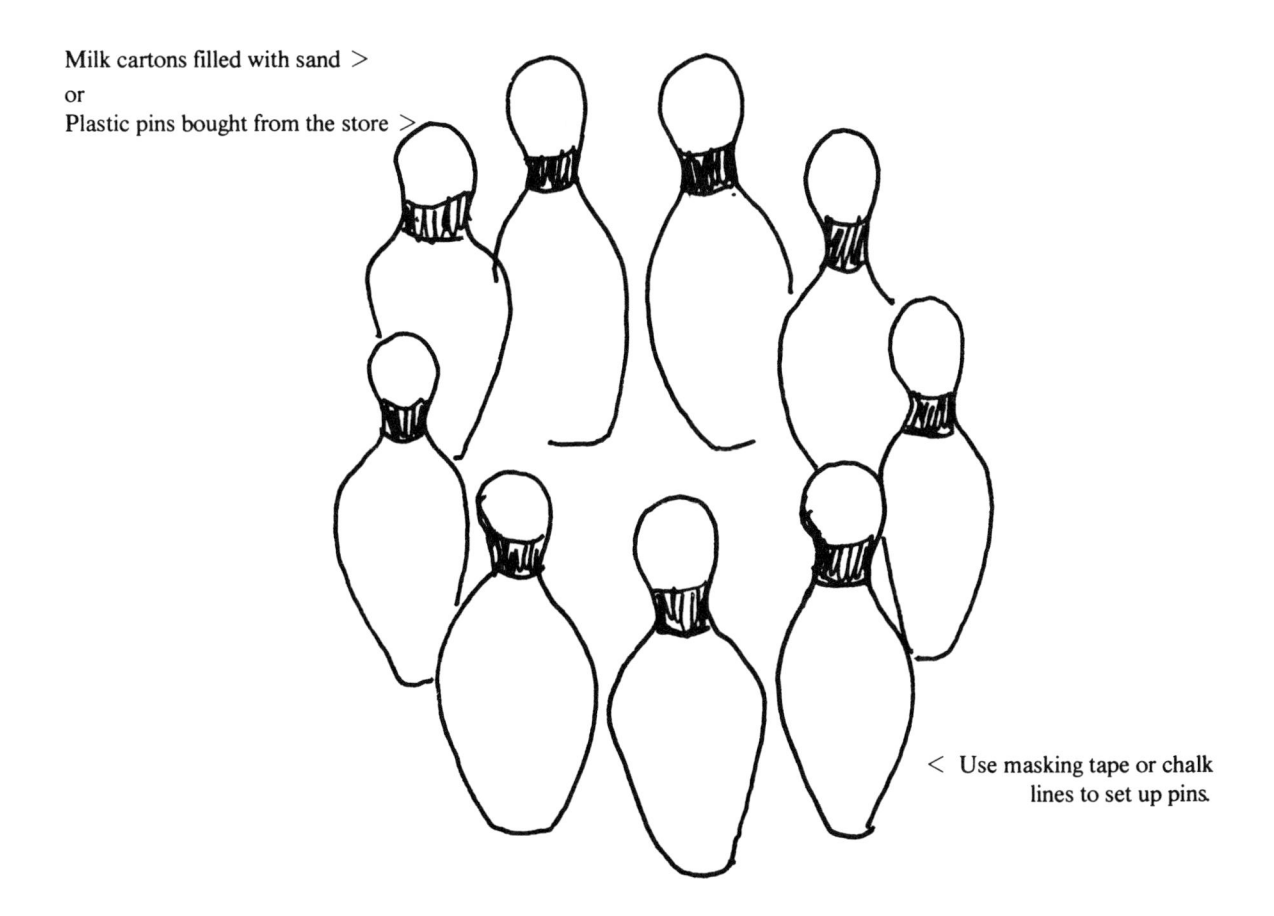

< Use masking tape or chalk lines to set up pins.

Birthday Round Up

< Invitation message on saddle

Birthday Round Up

Ages: 5-10 years

Invitations:

Make a picture of a bucking bronco. Write the party information on the saddle. Include in the message that guests should wear cowboy clothes and bring along a jump rope.

Decorations:

Corral — Create the look of a corral on the recreation room or outside play area. Place chairs in a circle with seat facing outward. String a clothesline around chairs. Complete the scene with items like bales of hay, stick horses, guitars, cowboy hats, boots, etc.

Table — Cover a board plank or table with brown butcher paper. Cut and decorate place mats to resemble cowboy hats.

Cacti Place Cards — Cut two cacti, 5 inches tall, out of heavy green paper. Slit one piece down from top to middle and the other from bottom to middle. Slide together and cacti will stand. Hang name tags from the cacti branches.

Centerpiece — Use Tinkertoys, the lid of a shoe box, and construction paper to create a covered wagon.

Nut Cups — Cut a cowboy boot shape out of construction paper. Decorate, then attach to nut cup.

Placemats — Use a 12-by-18-inch piece of construction paper. "Brand" each mat by using child's initials.

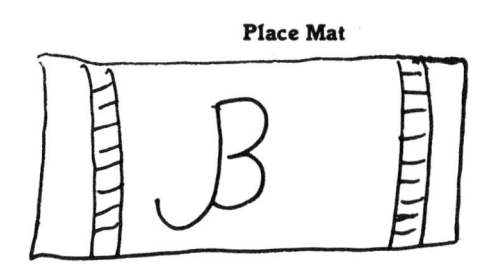

Place Mat

Menu and Recipes:

Cowboy Joes
---
1 lb. hamburger · ½ cup catsup
1 small onion diced · 1 teaspoon mustard
salt and pepper (optional)

Fry hamburger and onion, season to taste with salt and pepper. Drain well. Add catsup and mustard, mixing well. Simmer for 5 minutes and serve on hamburger buns.

Lonesome Salad
---
1 quart shredded cabbage · 1 teaspoon celery seed
1 teaspoon salt · ½ cup mayonnaise
1 tablespoon sugar · 1 tablespoon cider vinegar

Combine all ingredients and mix thoroughly. Chill.

Little Doggie Cake — Bake two chocolate sheet cakes using Anna's best cake chocolate variation, your favorite recipe or packaged mix. After baking, cut and assemble pieces according to the illustration below. Frost with vanilla and chocolate frosting. (Just add powdered cocoa to frosting recipe until desired shades of brown are obtained).

Little Doggie

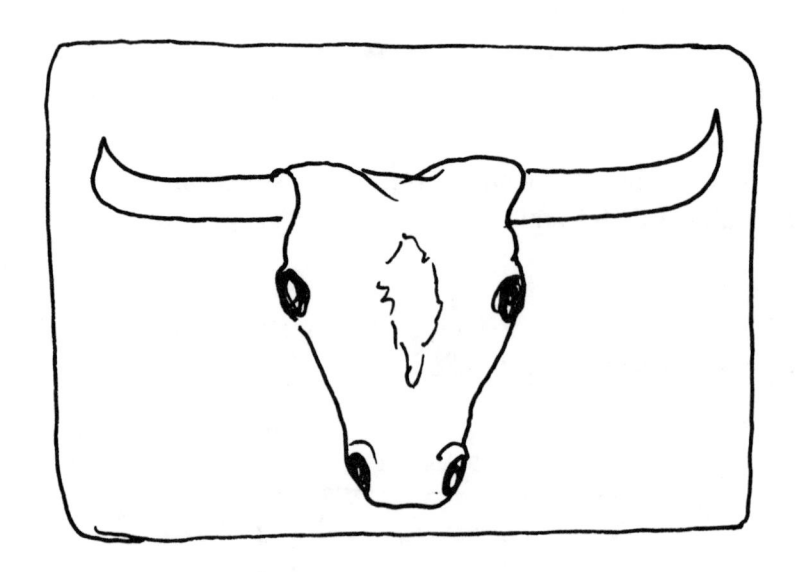

Activities:

Bandanas

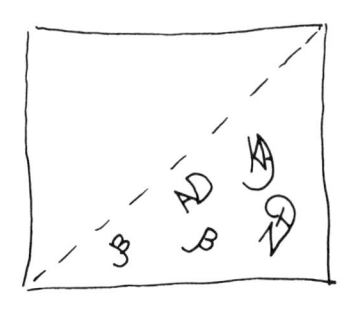

Bandanas — As guests arrive, provide each with a 12-inch square of plain cloth. Using magic markers, decorate bandana with symbols and their initials as brand. Wear bandanas during the party.

Round Up Those Cows — Choose two children to be cowboys. Provide each with a soft sponge or Nerf ball. The remaining children pretend to be cattle roaming freely on the range. At the signal the cowboys try to round up cattle by hitting them with a sponge. When the running cattle are caught they must sit down on a corral seat.

Pony Wagons — Children divided into pairs. "Hitch" one child by putting a rope around his waist or under arms. The other child pretends to be the driver and holds onto the ends of the rope. At the signal "giddy up," the pony wagon starts to gallop along the trail. (Rather than a race why not play a record so children can gallop to rhythmic beat).

Bucking Broncos — Child squats on a mat with his hands placed in front of him. At the signal, he tries to kick up his heels while balancing on hands. If a mat is not available use a large beach towel to define "kicking space."

Wheelbarrows — Divide children into pairs. (Partners should be nearly the same size). Mark two lines 30 feet apart. Line partners up at starting line. One child walks on hands while partner holds his feet. When they reach the end of the line they are to change roles and come back to the starting place. First team back wins. If space is limited, teams could take turns going one at a time while an adult times them. The team to make it in the shortest time is the winner.

Fastest Shooter in the West — Mark a target area on the floor. Have children stand in a semi-circle about 3 feet out from the target. Give each player a colored rubber band. Ask the children to hold the bands like sling shots and shoot. Award a prize to the child whose rubber band is nearest to the target.

Rope Jumping — Provide each guest with a rope. Be sure they are spaced away from each other. Have a contest to see who can jump the highest, do the most jumps with two feet, do the most on alternate feet, etc.

Rope Jumping

Lasso Twirling Contest — Provide each child with a rope. Tie tails of crepe paper at one end of short rope or in middle of longer rope. Have the children try twirling the rope clockwise and counterclockwise with both dominate and nondominate hands. Then let them try to twirl two ropes at once. They can also try to swing rope in various positions such as overhead or near ground. Provide a record with western swing music to add rhythm to twirls.

A Day with Cowboy (Birthday Child's Name) — Children sit in circle. The leader starts a story about cowboy by stating one sentence and starting another. (For Example: "Early one summer morning, Cowboy rose at daybreak. He could smell the _____.") The next child completes the sentence, then starts another sentence to add to the story. Continue telling the story until each child has had a turn. The birthday child then finishes the story. It's fun to tape the story, then play it back for the players to hear.

Rig-A-Jig-Jig — Children stand in a circle. One child is chosen to skip around the circle while all sing the verse. At the word "friend" the child selects a partner. The two gallop around the circle while all sing the verse. The game is repeated with each child selected as the partner taking the next turn at skipping around the circle as the verse is sung.

> *Verse:* As I was walking down the street, down the street, down the street
> A nice young friend I chanced to meet, Hi-Ho, Hi-Ho, Hi-Ho.
>
> *Chorus:* A rig-a-jig-jig and away we go, away we go.
> A rig-a-jig-jig and away we go, Hi-Ho, Hi-Ho, Hi-Ho.

Singing Circle Game — Buy or borrow from the library records that have music and directions for games like: Hokey Pokey, Looby Lou, Miller Boy, Farmer in the Dell, Mulberry Bush, and Skip to My Lou.

Singing Time — A few minutes before guests leave for home sing together some cowboy favorites such as "Get Along Little Doggies," "Skip to My Lou" or "Clementine." Records can be used but it is a delight to have the accompaniment played on a guitar.

Japanese Birthday Tea Party

Japanese Birthday Tea Party

Ages: 4-8 years (girls)

Japanese Landscape

Invitations:

Japanese Landscape Design — Mix tempera paint with a little water to thin the consistency. Drop a small blob of paint on the front fold of paper. Use a drinking straw and blow the paint blob into an interesting form. Add colors or let colors overlap. Complete invitation using a black pen to highlight or finish pictures formed by paint.

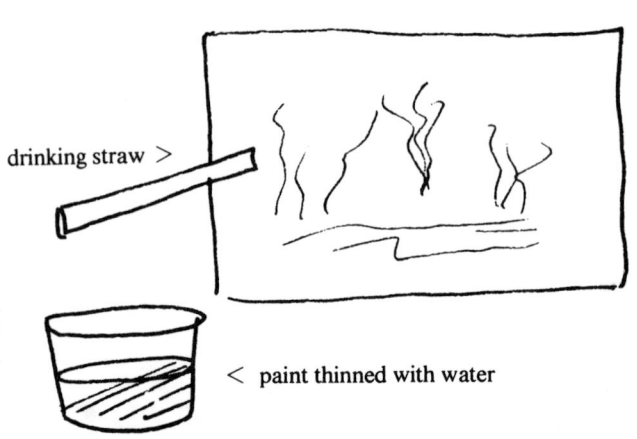

drinking straw >

< paint thinned with water

Decorations:

Butterfly, Bird, and Flower Mobile — Fold two pieces of black paper in half. Make a duplicate set of shapes while paper is still folded. Cut interesting windows in shapes. Select pieces of colored cellophane or tissue paper which are just a bit smaller than outer margin of shape. Brush the bottom shape with rubber cement, then lay the cellophane piece over it. Press down to be sure cement adheres. Brush the top shape with rubber cement, then press on top of cellophane. (The colored layer is sandwiched between the black layers and adds color to the windows.) Punch a hole at top. Hang the pretty shapes with string from a hanger or from pieces of twigs.

Lanterns — Fold a 12-by-18-inch sheet of paper in half, then in quarters. Cut out half forms of flowers, butterflies, and leaves on folds. Unfold. Paste a piece of cellophane or tissue paper under the paper. Staple or paste edges together to form a lantern shape. Add a handle made with crepe paper or ribbon.

Japanese Lantern

Crystal Garden — Several days before the party assemble a flat pan, some pieces of charcoal, ½ cup water, ½ cup salt, ½ cup liquid bluing, 1 cup ammonia, a few drops of blue, green, and yellow food coloring, a mixing bowl, and a plastic spoon. Place enough pieces of charcoal to cover bottom of pan. Mix water, salt, bluing, and ammonia in the bowl. Carefully pour over the charcoal. Make sure all pieces of charcoal get wet. Squirt a few drops of food coloring (except red) over the charcoal. Watch the garden grow. A small pagoda made by stacking boxes of diminishing sizes and covered with foil can be set in the garden.

Crystal Garden Centerpiece

< a boxed pagoda could be added

Japanese Table — Make a table that is no more than 18 inches high with bricks and a board or a cardboard box. Cover with a pretty pastel tablecloth. Use the crystal garden or add an elegant vase filled with real flowers as centerpiece. Place cushions or pillows on the floor around table for seats. If a miniature porcelain tea set is available, why not use it with these ladies?

Butterfly Napkin Rings and Place Cards — Draw and cut out lovely butterflies of pastel colors. Paste on a ring for the napkin holder or on a card folded in half as place cards.

Menu and Recipes:

Japanese Fold-Ups

1 bunch of green onions, minced
4 cloves of garlic, minced
1½ lb. ground beef
1 egg
2 tablespoons sesame oil
¼ cup soy sauce
1 package won ton skins
vegetable oil (for frying)
¼ cup rice vinegar

Combine onions, garlic, and ground beef; mix well. Add egg and ¼ cup soy sauce to beef mixture; mix well. Place 1 tablespoon beef mixture in center of each won ton skin; fold into a triangle, pressing edges to seal. Fry in ¼ inch oil over medium heat until beef is done, turning to brown both sides. May deep fat fry, if desired. Combine ⅔ cup soy sauce, vinegar and sesame oil; mix well. Serve with Japanese fold-ups.

Crispie Rice Squares

5 cups Rice Krispies
4 cups mini-marshmallows
¼ cup margarine or butter

Melt margarine in a 3-quart sauce pan, the add marshmallows and cook over low heat until melted. Add Rice Krispies and mix until well coated. Press into greased 9-inch-by-13-inch cake pan. Cool and cut into squares.

Fortune Cookies

4 egg whites
1 cup sugar
½ cup melted butter
½ cup flour
¼ teaspoon salt
½ teaspoon vanilla
2 tablespoons water

Write fortune messages on strips of paper. Mix sugar and egg whites. Beat until fluffy. Melt butter, then let it cool. Add flour, salt, vanilla, water, and butter to the sugar mixture. Beat until the batter is smooth. Pour batter from a spoon onto a greased cookie sheet. Form circle no larger than three inches in diameter. Bake at 375° for about 8 minutes. Before cookies are cool lay the messages on each circle. Fold circle in thirds, then bend the fold gently in middle.

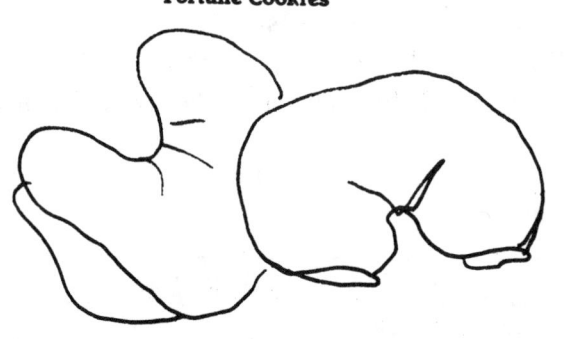

Fortune Cookies

You will meet a prince!

Butterfly Salad — Use the lettuce leaf as base. Body can be half a banana cut lengthwise. Wings are pineapple slices. Antennae can be pimento strips with ripe olives at tip.

Fresh Fruit — Strawberries and slices of mandarin oranges set out for goodies.

Fruit Tea — Combine 1 cup boiling water, two tea bags, ½ cup sugar, 4 cups ice water, ½ cup lime juice, and 2½ cups orange juice.

Activities:

Japanese Hopscotch — Place ten sticks in a row, about 1 foot apart. Take turns jumping over sticks and picking up sticks. On forward trip the player jumps over sticks with two feet. On return, she tries to hop on one foot, then balance on that same foot while picking up sticks along the way.

Japanese Tag — The player selected to be "It" chases others. When a player is tagged she must hold the spot touched and at the same time try to catch another player. Game continues until all children have been tagged.

Japanese Kimonas — Cut white paper or muslin in the form suggested. Each child can decorate her kimona with crayons or magic markers. Complete the outfit with a lovely crepe paper ribbon sash.

Japanese Kimono

< white paper or muslin

< pretty ribbon

Rice Relay — Place a bowl of rice at the far end of the play area. At the starting line for the game place two empty bowls. Children divide into two teams. The lead child in each team is given a spoon. At the "go" signal she runs to the filled rice bowl, fills spoon with rice, then returns to dump rice in the empty bowl. If rice spills, the player must return to the filled bowl for another spoonful. Continue the game for 2 minutes. At the "stop" signal, measure amount in each bowl to determine which team won!

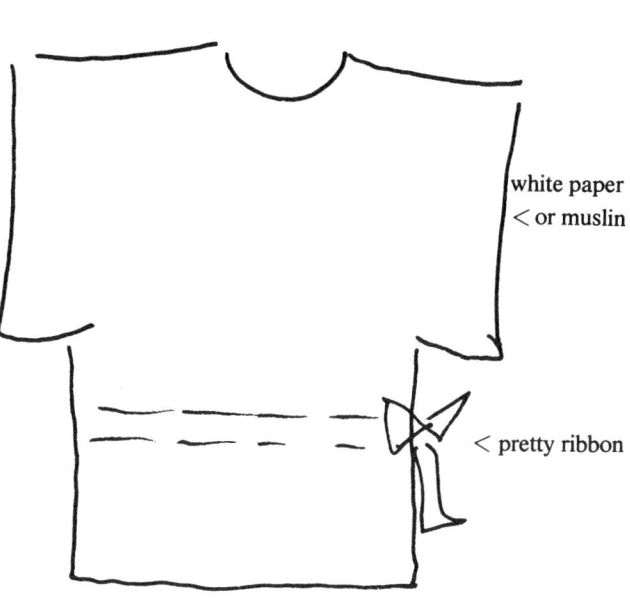

Balloon Volley Ball — Set up a low net in the play area before the party. Make rackets as described in Water Carnival Party. (For safety be sure to cover the top of the handle with masking tape). Inflate several balloons. Children divide into teams and stand on opposite sides of net. Toss a coin to determine the team to serve first. Each player on the serving team taps a balloon over the net with a racket. The players on the opposite team quickly try to tap it back. A point is made by opposite team each time a balloon hits the ground.

Japanese Fans — Use a piece of paper approximately 18 inches by 10 inches. Decorate. Fold widths into accordian pleats. Spread at top for fan, but keep bottom of pleat together with a staple or tape.

Japanese Fan

18-inch by 10-inch paper with accordian folds >

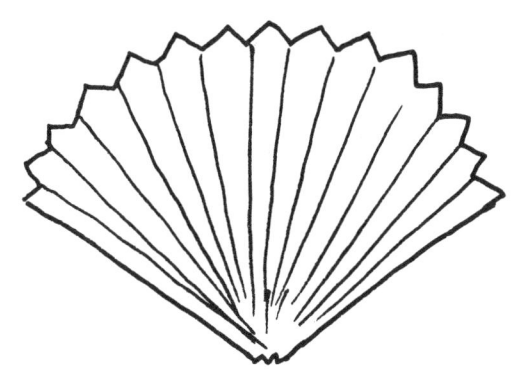

Mexican Patio Birthday Party

Mexican Patio Birthday Party

Ages: 7-11 years

Invitations:

Decorate the front of invitation with the theme picture of a Mexican dancer or create a colorful sombrero.

Decorations:

Patio — Remove or cover with sheets most of the furniture in patio or party area. Decorate background with pottery, wicker baskets, green potted plants and bright bouquets of flowers. Seats can be sturdy boxes covered with towels. Complete the setting with an Oje de Dios, bright paintings, pinatas, and Mexican curios.

Table — Cover with white paper. Run strips of several colors of coordinated crepe paper down center.

Placemats — Cut crepe paper of selected color scheme into circles 14 inches in diameter. Fold in half, then again into fourths. Use scissors to make notches of various shapes and sizes along folds and edge.

Napkins — Roll the napkin into a long roll. Fold in half, then stick into cup.

Bird Place Cards — Make a double form of the bird illustration on a piece of 8-by-11-inch colored construction paper. On small white circles write the letters of child's name. Paste circles on bird. Use a 6-by-18-inch strip of lightweight paper for wings. Fold in accordian pleats. Fan open at top, but staple bottom together. Make the tail in same manner, but use a shorter piece of paper. Staple both the bird wings and tail between bird forms. Glue or fasten together. Fold out feet flaps and fasten with staples or glue to a heavy cardboard base.

Flowering Tree Centerpiece — Fill a plastic cup with plaster of Paris or play dough. The stem, a wooden dowel or strip, is painted, then placed into a cup. Add painted popsicle branches. Complete with crepe paper leaves and flowers created out of egg carton cups or paper muffin tins.

Mexican Girl's Costume

Costumes (Girls) — Cut crepe paper into two rectangular bands, approximately 14 inches by 30 inches. Glue in crosscross fashion for a collar. Fringe by making 2-inch strips into edges.

Costumes (Boys) — Fringe the edges of a rectangular piece of crepe paper, approximately 20 inches by 40 inches. Cut a diamond hole in the middle for the head to pass through. Jorongos can be decorated with strips of contrasting colored crepe paper.

Oje de Dios (Eye of God) — Make this Mexican Indian good luck piece by using two popsicle sticks. Cross sticks, then secure by tying knots in yarn. Weave yarn over one stick and under next. To change colors, tie a new piece of yarn to one of the sticks. Guests may wish to make small Oje de Dios upon arrival at party.

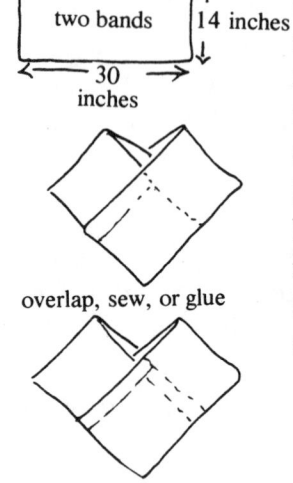

two bands — 14 inches — 30 inches

overlap, sew, or glue

Mexican Boy's Costume

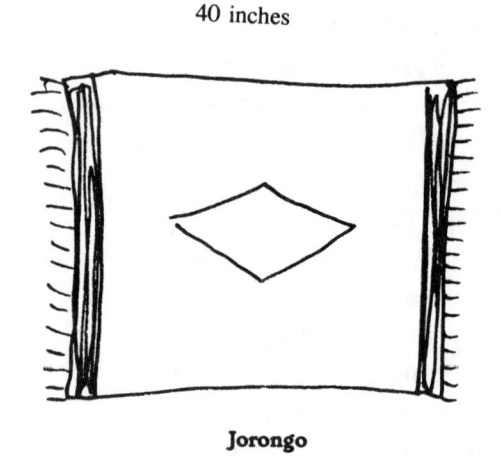

Jorongo — 40 inches — 20 inches

Oje de Dios – Eyes of God

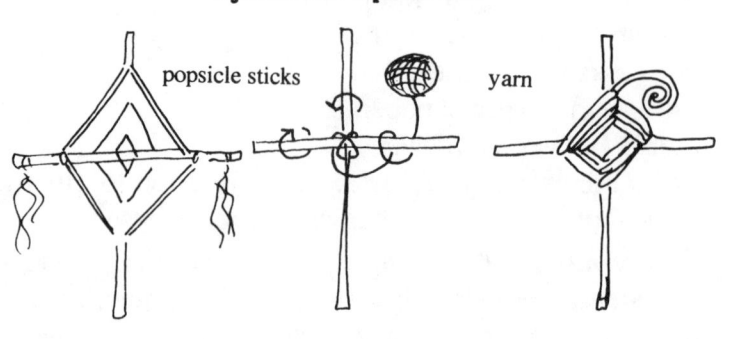

popsicle sticks   yarn

Menu and Recipes:

Tacos — Taco shell filled with refried beans, ground beef mixed with taco seasonings, shredded lettuce, and shredded cheddar cheese.

Raw Vegetables with Questo — Peel and cut raw vegetables into serving sizes. For extra crispness keep cool in ice water. Questo is made by mixing together 1 package of cream cheese, 3 tablespoons of milk, 1 cup shredded cheddar cheese, minced onion, garlic powder, and pinch of salt.

Hot Chocolate — Heat together slowly in saucepan 2 oz. unsweetened chocolate, ¼ cup sugar, pinch of salt, 1 teaspoon cinnamon, and 1 quart milk. When chocolate has melted, remove from heat, and beat until foamy.

Mexican Cream Cake

1 angel food cake
1 pint chocolate ice cream
1 pint vanilla ice cream
2 tablespoons powdered chocolate drink mix
4 to 6 tablespoons powdered sugar
1 pint whipping cream
½ cup toasted slivered almonds

Slice ½ inch thick layer from top of cake. Set aside. Hollow out cake, leaving ½ inch thick sides. Alternate layers of chocolate and vanilla ice cream, filling cake shell to top. Replace top slice; press gently to secure to ice cream. Whip cream until stiff, adding chocolate and sugar. Taste. Add more chocolate or sugar if needed. Frost cake with flavored whipped cream. Sprinkle with almonds. Place cake, uncovered, in freezer until cream is firm. (Cake will keep for several weeks in the freezer.)

Activities:

Basket Relay — Divide players into two teams. Provide each team with a basket with a flat base so it can be balanced on the head. At the signal "go" the first player of each team places the basket on head, then walks from starting line forward about 10 feet, walks around a chair or obstacle, then returns to the starting line. If the walk was successful and the basket did not fall off, pass on to the next player. However, if the basket is not balanced, the same player must start again. Continue for a set time. Hint: Younger children may take turns, but do not need to be in teams or a race. Older children may enjoy obstacles which require that they climb, turn, and twist, but still keep basket in place.

Eyes of the Great One — Before the party make two large eyes (grid boards) out of square boards that are 10½ inches on each side. Draw vertical and horizontal lines on these boards to form 1½-inch grids. Cut nine circles, 1¼ inches in diameter, and nine more that are ¾ inches in diameter. Make two small eyes (squares) for each guest; each side of these squares measures 3½ inches. Cut enough circles so that each guest can have a container filled with nine circles, ½-inch diameter; nine circles, ⅜-inch diameter; and nine circles, ¼-inch diameter.

To play: Explain that this is a game that requires keen observation. Pass out small grids and boxes containing circles. Invite players to take seats approximately 10 feet in front of where the great eyes are standing. Turn great eyes away from players and with pins or masking tape place several circles on grid squares. Turn great eyes so that players can concentrate for about two minutes on the pattern placement of circles. Reverse great eyes again. Players use their circles and try to match the patterns of great eyes on their eye grids. Hint: The players will need one or two trial runs to understand the game, but then will probably want to play it several times. For younger children it may be necessary to use only one grid and circles of one size only.

Mexican Ball Race — Provide each player with a small rubber ball or one made with wadded paper covered with masking tape. Players take position at the starting line. At the signal "go" they must continually kick their ball while racing to the finish line.

Mexican Dance — Play a festive Mexican record. Players, divided into pairs, face each other and join hands. During the verse, they hop on left foot and kick out with right, then reverse foot pattern. At start of chorus, hook right arms together and skip around in circle. Repeat actions or add variations such as clapping hands of partner.

Pinata Birthday Game — Make an animal pinata by first inflating a balloon. Next, cover the balloon with a ¼-inch layer of strips of newspaper dripping wet with liquid starch. Leave a hole 2 inches in diameter at the top of the balloon. When the papier mache is dry, paint it with tempera paint. After the paint has dried, pop and remove the balloon and fill the papier mache shell with goodies and confetti. Add arms, legs, and face made out of construction paper. Then, suspend the pinata from a tree limb. Blindfold the birthday child. He uses a broom handle or cardboard tube to try to hit the pinata stationed above him. (Be sure all guests are a safe distance away). Guests can take turns being blindfolded and trying to break the pinata. When it breaks the candy can be shared as treats.

Dancer, Dancer, Where Are Your Castanets? — Choose one child to be the Mexican Dancer. This child goes out of the party area or turns eyes away from the group. The castanets are hidden in pockets, under clothing or in hands of one of the players. The dancer skips around players trying to guess which one has stolen the castanets.

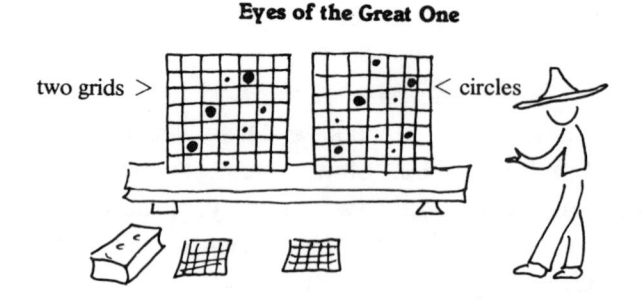

Eyes of the Great One

Chinese Dragon Party

Chinese Dragon Party

Ages: 6-10 years

Invitations:

Dragon Message — Make a double copy of the dragon design on green construction paper. Decorate the form with bits of foil, metallic paper, buttons, etc.

Decorations:

Dragon Cave — Drape sheets over chairs and card table to form the entrance and cave of a dragon's home. Place a stuffed animal dragon or one made out of boxes inside the cave.

Box Sculpture Dragon Centerpiece — Collect several boxes, most about shoebox size. Cover with green tissue paper. Fasten boxes together. Decorate with foil, ribbon, and paper.

Mini Dragon — Cut green egg cartons into lengthwise sections of six cups. Paste foil triangles on five egg cup backs to represent spines. Use pipe cleaners or paper strips as fiery tongue. On front cup add other features like button eyes and nose rings. When completed, place in front of each plate.

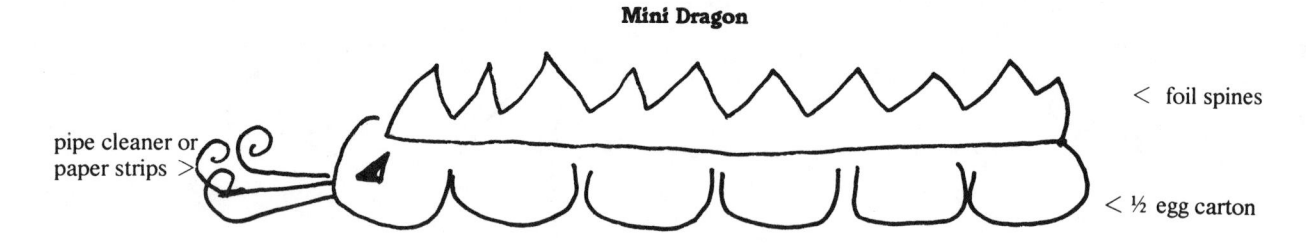

Mini Dragon

pipe cleaner or paper strips >

< foil spines

< ½ egg carton

Menu and Recipes:

Chinese Fried Rice — Stir fry favorite vegetable with small pieces of chicken. Serve on a bed of rice.

Fire Water — Dissolve in 1½ cups boiling water one 3-oz. package of orange gelatin and one 3-oz. package of lemon gelatin. Chill until thick, then beat in 1 pint of orange sherbet. Chill again. Fold in one 11-oz. can of drained mandarin oranges. Pour into mold. Chill until firm.

Dragon Cake — Bake two cake mixes in rectangular pans. Cool. Cut in sections as directed. Place the cake pieces in position on a large piece of cardboard covered with foil. Tint frosting pale green. Frost one cake section at a time. Use back of spoon to create the look of scaly skin. Shape licorice in curves for "fire" by placing them in the oven for a few minutes to soften, then bending them into shape. Decorate as follows: eyes out of orange rings with raisins or M & Ms, nose spots with red gumdrops, spines out of candy corn, and the fiery tongue with red licorice.

Dragon Cake

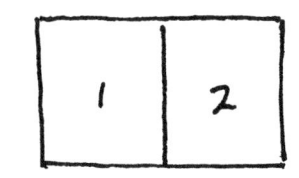

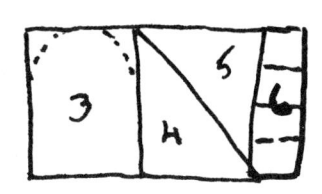

1-2 body
3- head
4- neck
5- tail
6- feet

Bake cake in two rectangular pans.

Activities:

Arrival — Dragon Puppet. Cut the top off of an 8-oz. milk carton. Cut to bottom from center on two opposite sides of carton. Fold in center bottom to form mouth. Decorate by overlapping green tissue paper circles to represent scales. Complete the puppet by adding foil teeth, button eyes, and piece of flannel for fiery red tongue. The dragon can "talk" when child moves mouth by opening and closing the fingers and thumb holding puppet.

Dragon Puppet

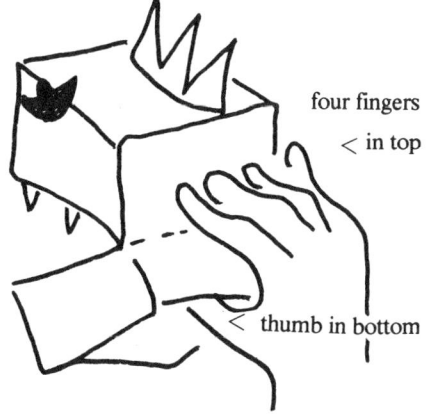

four fingers
< in top

< thumb in bottom

Touch the Dragon — One child who is chosen to be the dragon stands with back to others. The remaining children stand at the baseline about thirty feet away. Children advance toward the dragon while he counts rapidly to ten. At the count of ten the dragon turns to face the chidren. They instantly "freeze" because the dragon sends anyone moving back to the base line. The dragon turns around and the game continues. The first child to reach the dragon is the winner.

Catch the Dragon Tail — Divide children into groups of two or three. The first player in each group has his hands free. Each of the other players places his hands on the waist of the person in front of him. Tie a towel or cloth ribbon at the waist of the last player. The "dragons" must maneuver their line quickly and try to catch the tail of another dragon. When caught they "link" to form a larger dragon.

Puff the Magic Dragon — Sing along and dramatize the actions that fit the words of the record.

Giants and the Dragon — Children divide into two teams. Designate with pieces of rope the boundary lines of the giants' castle and home territory of the dragons. Toss a coin to determine which team will be the first to invade the territory of the other. The "home" team pretends to be thinking about something else while the "invaders" quietly approach their territory. If dragons are home team they listen for the leader's signal, "The giants are coming!" The dragons then run to catch as many giants as possible. Any giants tagged then join the dragon team. Hint: Be sure to establish rules of how to tag another player. Any rough action such as tackling or pushing takes the player out of the game.

Tangram Puzzles — (An authentic Chinese game). Make individual puzzles (see illustration) for each guest by drawing the pattern on each tag and cutting out the pieces. Children can either use the pieces and see how many designs (i.e., animal shapes, flowers, boats, etc.) of these they can make or they can try to reconstruct the square.

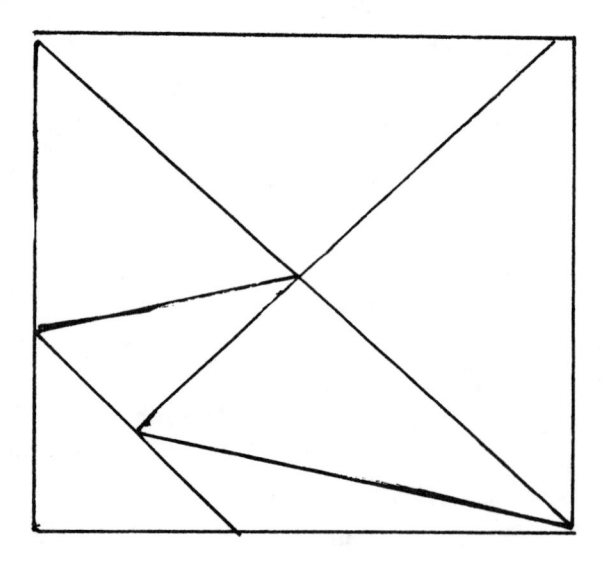

Tangram Puzzle

Hawaiian Luau Birthday

Hawaiian Luau Birthday

Ages: 6-10 years

Invitations:

A ukulele shape with the words "Aloha" and the child's name on the front. Place invitation message on the back.

Decorations:

Paper or real flowers.
Paper Chinese Lanterns — Make lanterns as illustrated and hang from the ceiling.
Table — Spread a length of bright print fabric on the floor. Adorn along the center with fresh flowers, gardenia leaves, cake, and fresh pineapple.
Place Cards — Ukulele with each child's name.

Menu and Recipes:

Stir Fried Chicken with Sweet and Sour Sauce — Skin, bone, and cut into small pieces an appropriate number of chicken breasts. Make marinade, using 1 or 2 tablespoons of soy sauce for each four chicken breasts. Marinate chicken pieces for at least three hours. Heat an electric skillet to 350°. When skillet is hot, add chicken and one onion sliced in rings. (Be careful of splattering.) Stir until chicken is almost white, and add 1 package of thawed frozen pea pods. Stir for 1 minute. Add 1 can of water chestnuts and 1 can of bamboo shoots. Serve with sweet and sour sauce.
Fresh Fruit — Fresh melon and pineapple
Beverages — Pineapple Delight Punch
Coconut Cake — Use white cake mix with coconut flavoring. Decorate as illustrated.

Coconut Cake

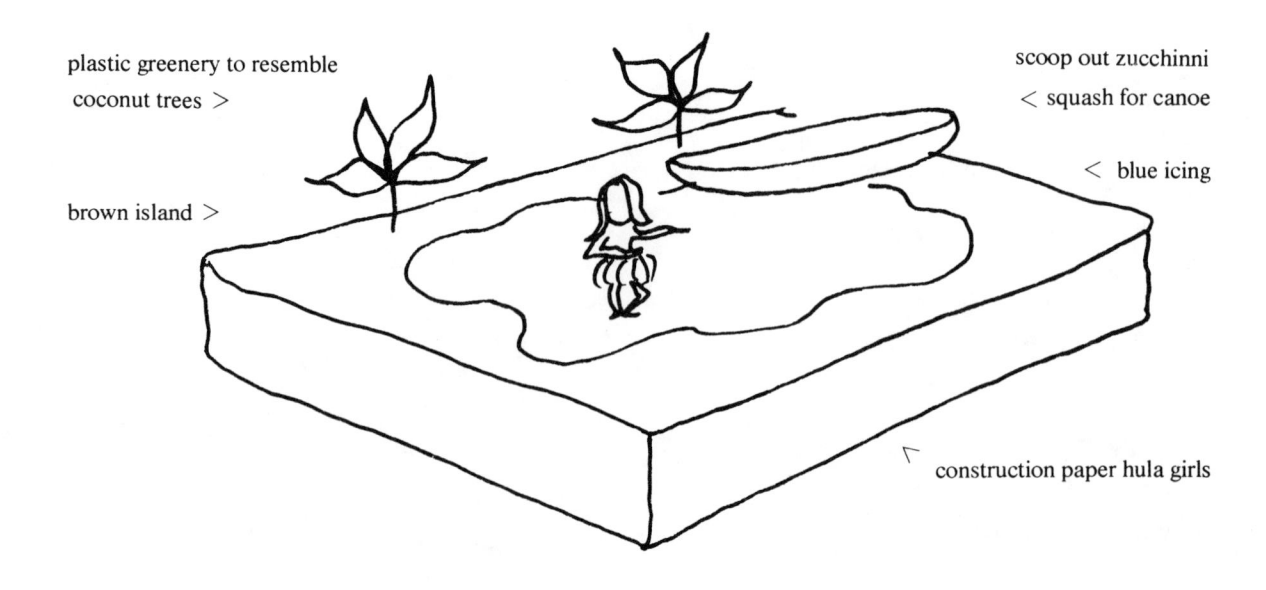

plastic greenery to resemble coconut trees >
brown island >
scoop out zucchinni < squash for canoe
< blue icing
construction paper hula girls

Activities:

Greeting — Make each guest feel welcome by placing a lei around his or her neck and saying, "Aloha."

Costumes — Girls make grass skirts with brown paper bags. Cut sacks open and remove bottom. Cut into strips, but leave about two inches intact at the top. Staple skirt onto ribbon that is long enough to tie around the waist. Headbands and swords can be part of the costume for the boys.

Table Mats and Sit Upons — Assist guest in making mats. Use 9-by-12-inch colorful construction paper for table mats. Fold. Start at the center and cut in several strips. Be sure to leave at least 1 inch at each end. Have 12-inch strips of paper available. Weave strips in and out of cut paper. Staple in place. Sit upons are made by the same method but with 12-by-12-inch brown butcher paper.

Authentic Hawaiian Folk Games

Pebble Race — Children stand at the starting line. Place 5 pebbles on the back of child's hand. He must try to run to the finish line and back without dropping any pebbles. Award prizes for those who don't drop any pebbles.

Oyster Shell Race — Draw two parallel lines about 10 feet apart. The territory between these lines is a neutral zone. Draw a goal line for each team about 40 to 60 feet away. Children are divided into two teams, one called light and the other dark. A leader of one team tosses an oyster shell (if one is not available use any object that has a light and dark side). If the shell falls dark side up then the light team runs for its goal and the dark side chases. If the light side falls, the roles are reversed. When a player is caught, he joins the captors. Play until most of the players are on one side.

Dancing the Hula — Play Hawaiian music. Invite the children to create a dance.

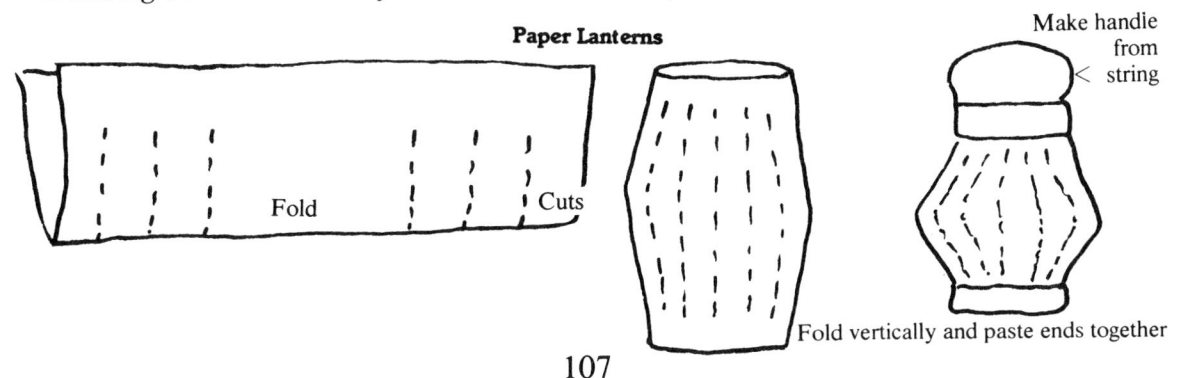

Construction Paper Hula Girl

popsicle stick

Paper Lanterns

Fold | Cuts

Fold vertically and paste ends together

Make handle from string

5

Birthdays Around the Calendar

Snowman's Birthday Party

Snowman's Birthday Party

Ages: 3-6 years

Invitations:

A snowman picture made by the birthday child on double fold of blue or gray construction paper.

Decorations:

Snowman — Make a large outline of a snowman on posterboard. Decorate by pasting on white Styrofoam packing disks. Add a hat, nose, and eyes.

Table — Cover with white tablecloth. At each place use a paper doily as a placemat. Make snowman place cards.

Menu and Recipes:

Snowman Place Cards

< popsicle stick

Styrofoam ball >

trim off bottom ∧
to make stable

Snowwiches — Use biscuits or cut circles out of slices of bread. Spread with pineapple and cream cheese. Use raisins to decorate.

Snowman's Garden — Use round vegetables such as cucumbers, carrot circles, tomatoes, and peas. Children make snowmen out of vegetables before eating.

Cheese Snowman — Shred cheddar cheese. Mix with tiny bits of minced onion. Moisten with mayonnaise. Roll into circles. Place three circles together to look like a snowman.

Snowballs — Place a scoop of crushed ice into a paper cup. Drizzle thawed concentrated fruit juice on top. Serve with straws and spoons.

Snowman Cake — Bake a favorite cake recipe in three round pans with 3-inch, 5-inch, and 8-inch diameters. Place baked cake circles on a sheet to form a snowman. Decorate cake with white icing and coconut. Chocolate icing can be used for outlines. Use cherries for mouth and raisins or chocolate cookies for eyes, nose, and buttons.

Activities:

Make Your Own Snowman — Make play dough with 2 cups of flour, 1 cup salt, and water to moisten. Stir into a ball. Knead 7 to 10 minutes until dough has a smooth, firm consistency. Store in an airtight container. Give children a round ball of play dough. They may shape with hands or use cookie cutters. Twigs or toothpicks may be added to represent arms.

Soapmen — Make soap paint by placing a small amount of detergent in a bowl, then beating with a mixer. Add a few drops of water to make bigger suds. Each child draws an outline of a snowman on a piece of dark paper. Add soap paint to the outline. Eyes, nose, and mouth can be added with watercolor magic marker or tiny pieces of construction paper.

Knock the Hat Off the Snowman — Draw the picture of a snowman on a large box. Place an old hat on the top. Children stand about 5 feet away from the snowman target and take turns trying to knock off the hat using bean bags, yarn, or string balls.

Build a Snowman — Paste circles of three different sizes and hats onto cards of posterboard or construction paper. Place cards, face side down, in a box or bowl. Children each receive a blank sheet of paper that represents snow-covered ground. The object of the game is to see who can build a snowman bottom up by drawing large to small circles, then a hat. If a player draws a small circle before getting the large circle, he must throw it back in the bowl. If he draws a hat before having his three sizes for snowman he must throw all cards back into bowl and start a new snowman.

Five Little Snowmen — Dramatize the following poem:

    Five little snowmen, happy and gay.
    First one said, "What a beautiful day."
    Second one said, "We'll never have tears."
    Third one said, "We'll stay here for years."
    Fourth one said, "But what will happen in May?"
    Fifth one said, "Look, we're melting away!"

Historical Heroes Birthday Celebration

Betsy Ross

Historical Heroes Birthday Celebration

Ages: 9-12 years

Invitations:
Silhouettes of Historical Heroes.

Decorations:
Table — Checkered tablecloth, pewter or earthenware dishes.

Place Cards — Yankee Doodle Soldiers. Collect cardboard tubes. Paint the top third white, the center red, and bottom black. Paint or use felt scraps for facial features. Use ball fringe for hat. Arms can be piece of construction paper glued to a tube. Belt and collar are pieces of gold trimming. Make band of white paper and attach with name of child.

Room — Use furniture and accessories representing Early America.

Place Cards

- < ball fringe
- < construction paper
- < paint face
- < belt of gold trim
- < name of child

white >
red >
black >

Menu and Recipes:
Ham

Cornbread or *Homemade Biscuits* — Serve with butter and maple syrup.

Honest Abe and Betsy Ross Salad (See illustrations.)

Honest Abe Salad
- carrot >
- olive >
- ¼ olive >
- egg >
- ½ olive >

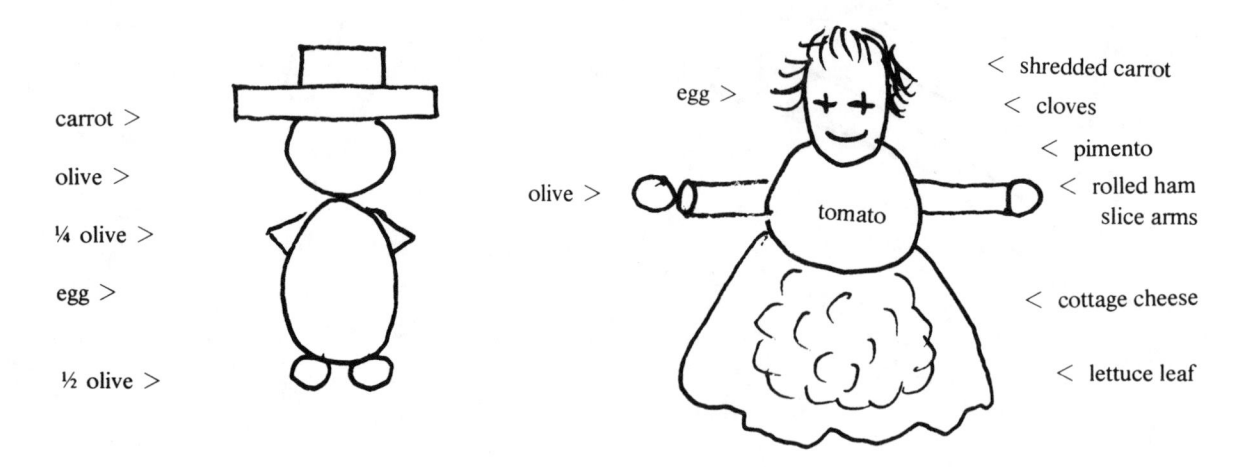

Betsy Ross Salad
- egg >
- olive >
- tomato
- < shredded carrot
- < cloves
- < pimento
- < rolled ham slice arms
- < cottage cheese
- < lettuce leaf

Drum Cake — Use devil's food or chocolate cake. Bake in round pans. Frost with white frosting. Decorate with peppermint candy canes around edge with maraschino cherry at top and base of each cane.

Activities:

Cooking — Children can make butter by using an old fashioned butter churn or by shaking cream in jars until it separates. Each guest should also make his own salad according to the directions.

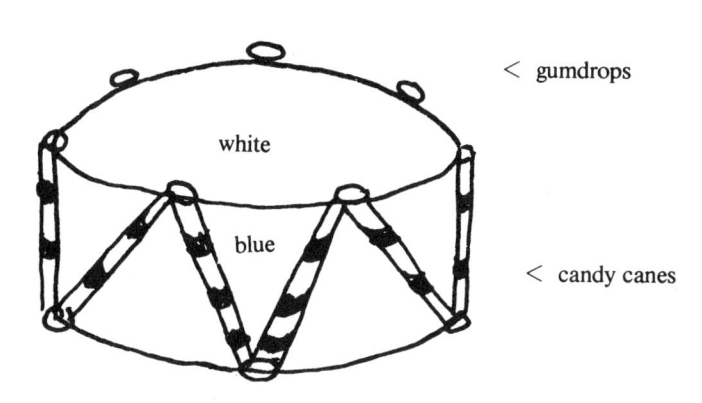

Are You There? — Collect an assortment of old clothes and wigs and have available construction materials such as doilies, cloth scraps, crepe paper, etc. On cards describe famous historical scenes such as the signing of the Declaration of Independence, the first Thanksgiving, or Paul Revere's ride. At the party divide children into teams. Each team selects a card with the scenario of an historical event. Allow about 10 minutes to make costumes and plan a short performance depicting the event. If children are older, the teams may depict actions of an historical occasion. Other teams try to guess the event.

George/Martha — Children join hands in a large circle. Choose a boy to be "George" and a girl to be "Martha." Blindfold George and stand him inside the circle. George calls out, "Martha," and she must answer each time, "George." He tries to catch her by listening to the direction of her voice. When George catches Martha he takes his place in the circle and chooses someone to take his place. The blindfold is placed on Martha who tries to catch the new George.

Back-to-Back Tag — Children divide in pairs and stand back to back. One child will be without a partner. At a signal each child must run and find another partner. The child who does not have a partner at the start tries his best to get a partner, thus making another child the odd player.

Race on Stilts — Collect several coffee cans. Punch two holes out of the bottom. Insert through holes a rope long enough so each end will reach the hands of the children. To race, each child stands on two coffee cans. At the signal "go" they try to quickly get to the finish line. (The walking on stilts is accomplished by pulling cans up with rope, which is held in the hands.)

Other Favorite Activities

Dance to *Looby Loo, Virginia Reel, Jimmy Crack Corn* (available on folk game albums).

Hearts and Flowers Birthday Party

Hearts and Flowers Birthday Party

Ages: 5-8 years

Invitations:

Cut three hearts of varying sizes and glue together from smallest to largest by gluing small beads between each heart.

Decorations:

Heart Mobile — Cut various sizes and colors of paper hearts. Hang from a line made of white yarn around the party room.

Table — Cover table with white tablecloth. Make placemats with large pieces of red paper cut into heart shape. Scallop edges and cut holes to create a doily effect.

Place Cards — Cut two small hearts, one white and one red, the same size. Glue a large doily to the back of the white heart. Cut a window in the red heart. Glue around the edges except for 1 inch, then attach hearts together. Write the child's name inside the window. Fold the bottom of the red heart forward and the bottom of the white heart backward so the card will stand.

Heart Place Mat

Hearts and Flowers Centerpiece — Cut various lengths of ¼-inch red strips of construction paper. Fold each strip in half and crease fold. Fold ends together to form a heart shape, then glue. Cut 3-by-5-inch index cards in ¼-inch lengthwise strips. Wrap each strip tightly around a pencil. Slide the curled paper off the pencil, then dip one edge into a small amount of glue. Place curl inside the heart shape. Repeat, making and gluing paper curls until each heart is filled. Wrap a red pipe cleaner around the end point of each heart, then place in piece of Styrofoam or oasis. To make flowers cut egg cups out of Styrofoam egg cartons. Flute edges. Stick a pipe cleaner through the bottom of the cup and secure by bending the end. Stick into Styrofoam or oasis. Complete by adding green leaves made with construction paper.

Hearts and Flowers Centerpiece

Place Cards

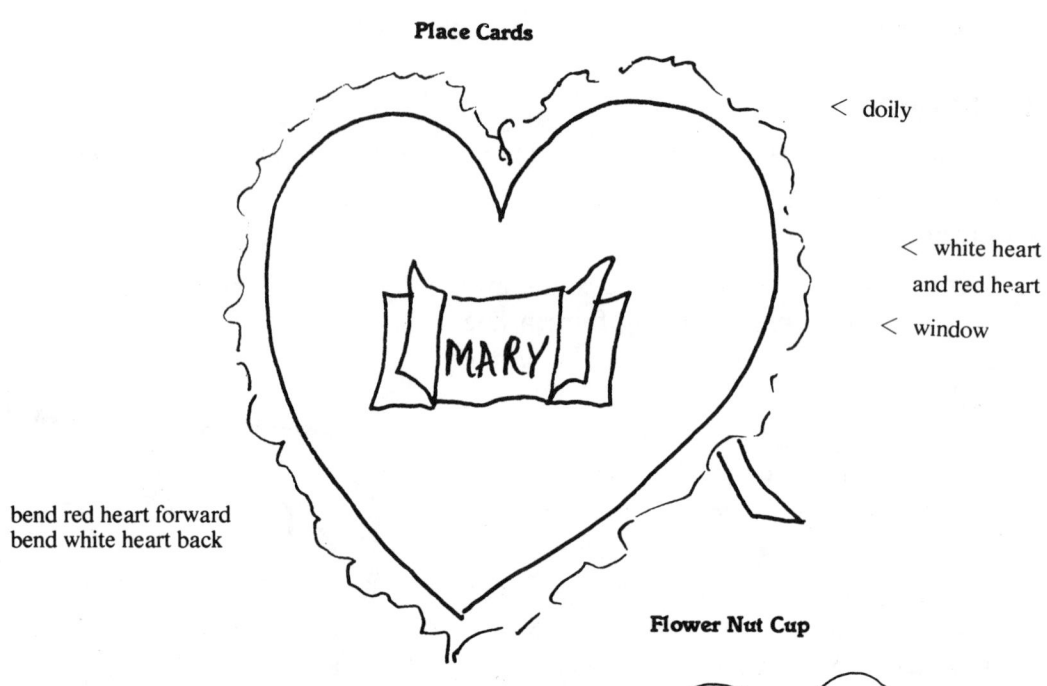

< doily

< white heart
and red heart

< window

bend red heart forward
bend white heart back

Flower Nut Cup

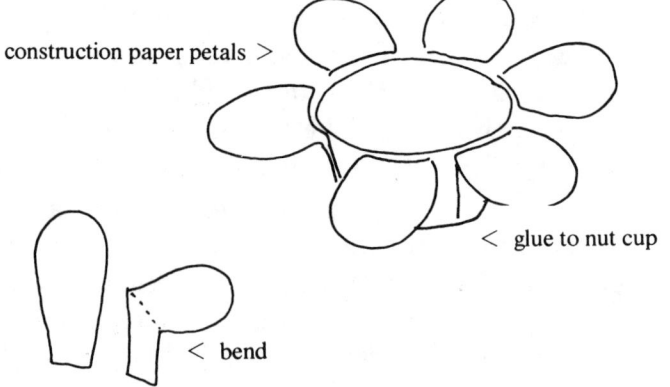

Flower Nut Cup — Cut petals out of construction paper. Petals should be two times the height of the nut cup. Staple, tape, or glue petals to cup with narrow tips at the top, then bend outward.

construction paper petals >

< glue to nut cup

< bend

Menu and Recipes:

Flower Salad — Spread slices of ham or bologna with cream cheese and roll up. Cut rolls into thirds and secure each piece with a toothpick. Cut American cheese slices into circles using a small circular cookie cutter. Place cheese in the center of a platter and arrange meat rolls around it. Add celery stick stem and leaves to complete flower.

Pink Fluff — Mix 12 oz. cottage cheese, 20 oz. can of well-drained crushed pineapple, 3 oz. box of cherry or strawberry flavored gelatin and 4 oz. frozen whipped cream topping in a bowl. Chill until ready to serve.

Candy Mint — Put ½ cup sweetened condensed milk, 1 box 10X confectioners' sugar, ½ teaspoon peppermint extract (or other flavoring), plus a few drops of red coloring in a bowl and mix well. Roll into small balls and flatten to look like flowers.

Heart Sherbet — Dissolve 1 3 oz. package cherry or strawberry Jello, 1 cup sugar, and 1 small package unsweetened powdered fruit drink in 2 cups of hot water. Add 2 cups of cold water. Mix well and pour into heart-shaped molds.

Heart Cake — Bake a strawberry cake or white cake mix that has been tinted pink in a heart-shaped cake pan. If that shape is not available use one 8-inch square pan and one 9-inch round pan. Put pieces together in heart shape and frost with whipped cream or frozen whipped topping. Sprinkle with little red hearts

Activities:

A Special Valentine — Prior to the party write each child's name on a small heart. Attach a string to each. Place the hearts inside a large heart-shaped envelope with strings extending from it. As children arrive they choose a string and pull out the heart attached to it from the envelope. Have markers and pencils available so that each child can decorate a valentine or write a verse for the name appearing on the heart. Pass out valentines later and have each recipient guess who made his valentine.

Best Friend Review — Request that each guest bring an unmarked envelope containing several of his baby pictures. Pass out envelopes during the party, making sure no one has his own pictures. Children take turns making up stories about the baby pictures in their envelope. As they finish can they guess which friend was the baby?

Drop Your Heart — Use a six inch paper heart. Children join hands and form a circle. To make the circle larger all should step backward until arms are fully extended. Drop hands and start the game. The child chosen to be "It" skips around the outside of the circle and drops the heart at heels of one of the players. If "It" is caught he continues in the same role. If he successfully reaches the spot vacated before being tagged, the next player takes over as "It."

Hit the Target — Make a large cardboard heart, then paint it red. Also make eight 5-inch hearts, four of one color and four of another out of a fuzzy fabric or Velcro. Glue the eight hearts onto the large heart. Be sure that the fuzzy side is facing out. Color eight ping pong balls with colors that match small hearts. Cover them with Velcro strips. Make sure the Velcro stiff side is facing out. To play divide the children into two teams. Give each team four balls. At "go" signal the first player of each team throws his four balls at the heart target. Score two points for each ball that sticks on matching colored fabric and one point for balls sticking to the other colored hearts. Add up the total team points after each member has had a chance to play.

Heart Steps — Cut four 12-inch hearts out of construction paper or posterboard. Divide guests into two relay teams and provide each team with two hearts. The lead player in each team must place the hearts on the floor "stepping stone fashion," and step only on the hearts as he races to a predetermined point and back. The hearts are then passed to the next team player.

Me and My Shadow — Divide the party guests into partners. The partners make two teams. Teams line up at a starting point. The first set of partners in each team is provided a ball. Their objective is to work together to carry the ball to a predetermined point, then back to finish line without dropping the ball. To complicate their task the partners must be back to back with elbows locked. They must carry ball without touching it with hands. If the ball is dropped, the players must return to the starting line and begin again.

Kite Party

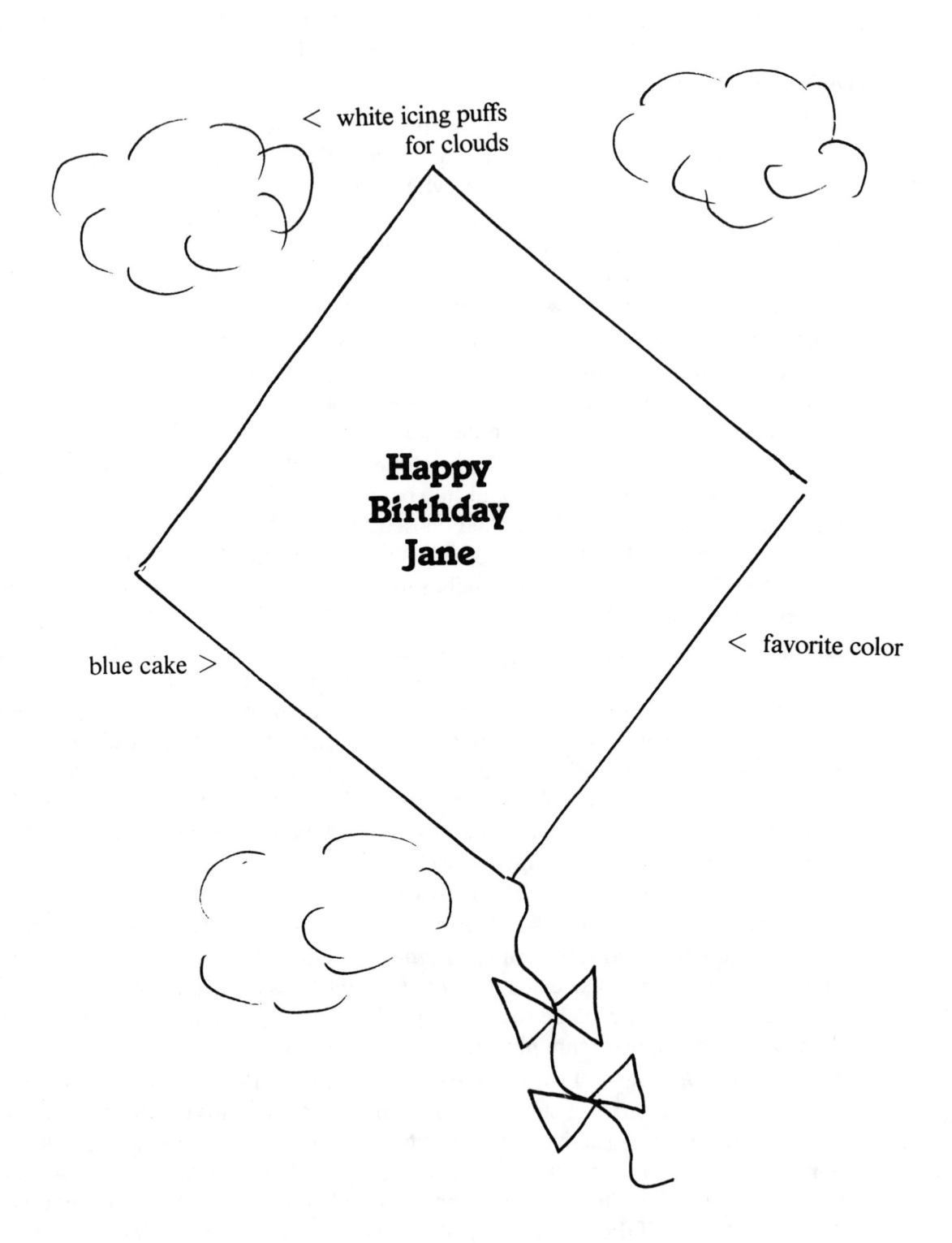

< white icing puffs for clouds

Happy Birthday Jane

blue cake >

< favorite color

Kite Party

Ages: 3-6 years

Invitations:
The birthday child decorates colorful construction paper kites. Place the message on the back of each kite.

Decorations:
Kite Mobiles — Hung around party area.

Kite Placemats and *Kite Napkins* — Made from miniature diamond-shaped paper.

Kite Place Cards — Straws with a miniature kite hooked at the top.

Menu and Recipes:
Kitewiches — Tuna salad served on diamond-shaped bread and outlined with cheese spread. Tail is celery and carrot sticks or strings of cheese.

Punch — An orange drink.

Kite Cake — Bake a sheet cake in a rectangular or square pan. Decorate with small triangle cookies.

Activities:
Kites — Have materials such as string, paper, scraps, construction paper, scissors, and glue ready to assemble. Soon after arrival of guests each child will make his own kite. When completed, take kites outside. Run, holding onto kite string. If there is any wind, the kites will fly behind running children.

Kites in a Tree — One child stands in place and pretends to be a tree. The other children are kites that fly in and around the tree. If the tree "tags" the kite the places are exchanged.

Catch a Tail — One child is "It." "It" chases other children. The first one caught joins hands with "It." Together they try to catch another child. Continue until the kite tail includes most of the children.

Buy a Tail — Two children are "kites." Each of the other players pick a colored strip of cloth or crepe paper. Tie the strip around waist. The "kites" take turns calling colors they want as part of their tail. When all the colors are attached the kites have a race.

Kites

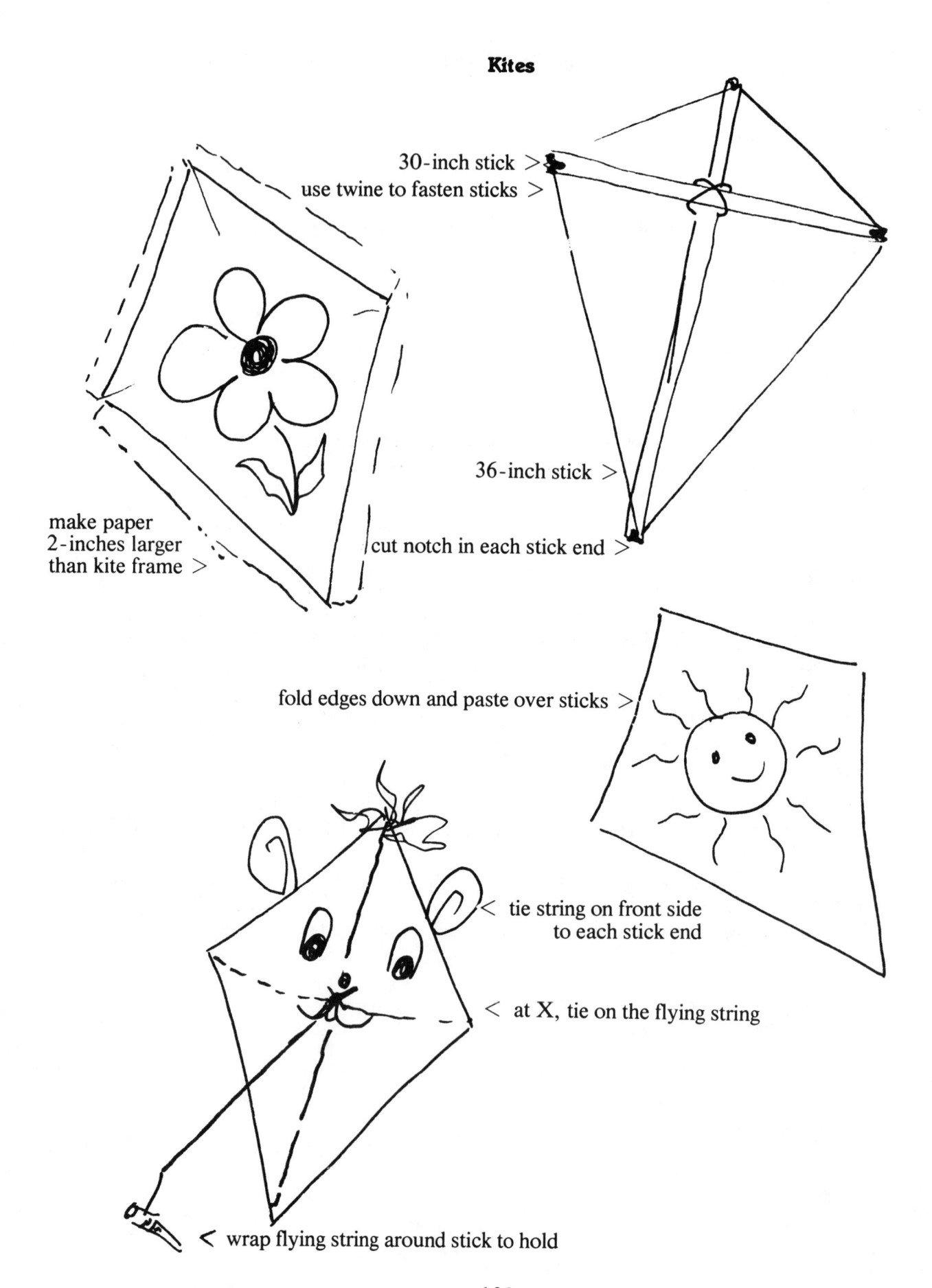

30-inch stick >
use twine to fasten sticks >

36-inch stick >

cut notch in each stick end >

make paper 2-inches larger than kite frame >

fold edges down and paste over sticks >

< tie string on front side to each stick end

< at X, tie on the flying string

< wrap flying string around stick to hold

April Fool's Backwards Birthday Party

April Fool's Backwards Birthday Party

Ages: 5-9 years

Invitations:

Picture of child with shoes on hands, mittens on feet, and hat and shirt on backwards. Write the message backwards. (Suggest a mirror be used to decipher. Message needs to explain that guests are to come to party with clothes on backwards).

Invitation

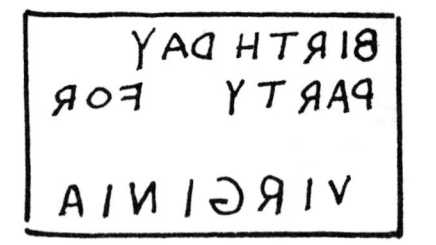

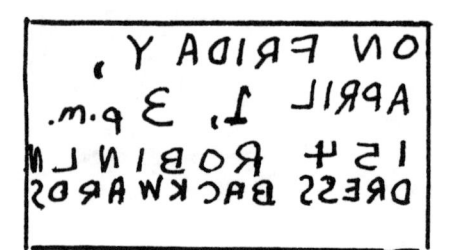

```
BIRTHDAY              ON FRIDAY,
PARTY FOR             APRIL 1, 3 p.m.
                      15th ROBIN LN
VIRGINIA              DRESS BACKWARDS
```
(shown mirrored/backwards)

Decorations:

Table — Have tablecloth with wrong side up. Place silverware on wrong side of plates. Place cups and glasses on front of plate, nearest to table edge.

Centerpiece — An upside down scene of houses, trees, and children

Door — Outline the form of birthday child on large brown paper. Cut out, color in clothes and features, then fasten on the door with feet up.

Room — Turn toys and dolls over, upside down, and topsy turvy.

Favors:

Bubble Gum — The kind with a squishy center.
Squirt Rings
Worm in Can
A Book That Won't Open

Menu and Recipes:

Mixed Up Rolls — Basic recipe with something squishy in center.

Humpty Dumpty Salad — Make like Honest Abe Salad in Historical Heroes. Place figures upside down.

Green Mashed Potatoes — Add a drop of green food coloring.

Ham Slices

Fizzies — A drink with ginger ale added at last minute so it will tickle the nose.

Pineapple Upside Down Cake — Place candles on completed cake so they stick out of side of cake or use the trick candles that cannot be blown out.

Pineapple Upside Down Cake

1¼ cup sifted all purpose flour	⅓ cup soft shortening
2 teaspoons baking powder	½ cup granulated sugar
¼ teaspoon salt	1 egg, unbeaten
3-4 tablespoons butter or margarine	½ cup syrup drained from pineapple
2 small cans pineapple rings	½ cup brown sugar

maraschino cherries (approx. 6)

Melt butter and cover 8-inch square or round pan. Sprinkle with brown sugar. Arrange pineapple rings on brown sugar mixture. Place a cherry inside of each. Sift flour, baking powder, and salt. Mix shortening with sugar until light and fluffy with electric mixer at medium speed. Then at low speed, beat in alternately the flour mixture and pineapple syrup. Spread batter carefully over pineapple rings. Bake at 375° about ¾ of an hour or until center comes out clean when tested with a toothpick. Remove from oven and cool 10 minutes. Carefully loosen cake from sides of pan. Invert serving plate onto pan, then flop so cake goes onto plate. Add any fruit that stuck by taking off with spatula and placing on cake.

Activities:

Arrival — Children arrive at party wearing clothes backwards or wrong side out. Plan for time to giggle and enjoy looking at each outfit. Greet each guest by saying, "Goodbye, we're happy you came." Guest must walk into room backwards.

Sign in Art — Provide bright colors of construction paper, scissors, pencils or markers, and glue. Fold a 9-by-12-inch piece of construction paper in half the long way. Use a pencil or marker to write name in cursive on fold. Try to write big with the bottom of letters touching the fold in paper. While paper is still folded cut outline and spaces between letters. Open, then paste this name design on a contrasting piece of construction paper.

Sign in Art

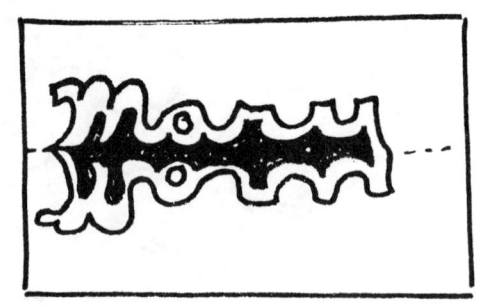

Backwards Simple Simon — Play like the original "Simple Simon" game except children mimic the reverse of the direction. For example, if Simple Simon says, "Sit down," the players stand. If children follow the directions correctly they goof.

Dress the Doll — Prepare an outline of a doll on a large piece of paper. Attach to a wall. Provide cut-outs of clothes such as a blouse, shirt, socks, gloves, necktie or scarf, belt or hat. Each player selects an article of clothing to place on the doll outline. (Attach a circular ring of masking tape to the back of each piece when child is ready for his turn). Take turns to be blindfolded and place place clothing piece on doll form. Continue until all children have had a turn. (There should be lots of giggles).

Backwards Relay Races — Children stand at starting line with back toward goal. At signal they race to finish goal by walking backward, running backward, jumping backward, crawling backward like a crawfish or walking on a line or rope backward.

April Fool Jokes — Supply several answers to jokes. The children give the questions.

Dress the Doll

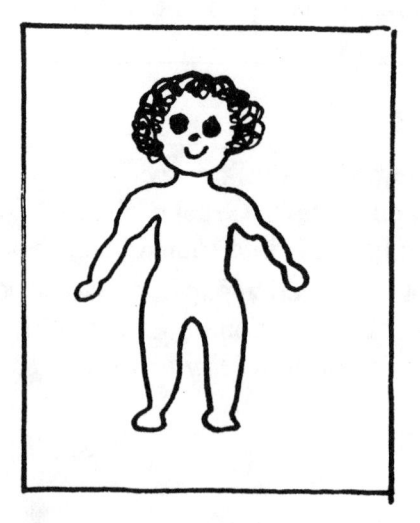

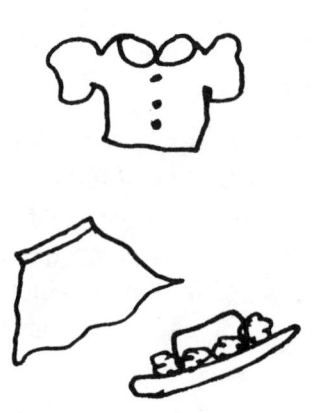

Spring Birthday Fest

Spring Birthday Fest

Ages: 3-7 years

Invitations:

Pop-Out Card — Fold a stiff piece of paper in half. Along edge of fold draw one half of a chick, bunny, duck, or egg. Place a tab at about the middle of the shape. Cut along lines except for tab. Open paper and color picture. Push the picture out from the paper and crease tabs. Paste this page onto another sheet. Decorate front cover and write a message on back.

Pop-Out Cards

- fold in half
- cut shape
- do not cut tab
- open paper
- color picture
- push picture out and crease tabs
- paste onto another sheet

Decorations:

Table — Cover table with a pastel tablecloth.

Egg-Shaped Placemats — Cut placemats from assorted shades of pastel construction paper and decorate with magic markers.

Spring Napkin Holder — Cut paper towel rolls into 2-inch lengths and color them with pastel magic markers or tempera paints. Cut miniature ducks, eggs, bunnies, chicks, etc. out of white paper and glue them around the ring.

Duck Treat — Fold a piece of yellow paper so that it measures approximately 11-by-4½-inches. On fold, snip cuts ½ inches apart and approximately 2 inches in depth. Trim tips of feathers. Drape this feathered portion over a nut cup, then glue in place. Make a double duck head. Fold back tabs and paste onto nut cup. Make orange webbed feet and glue along sides. Fill with goodies.

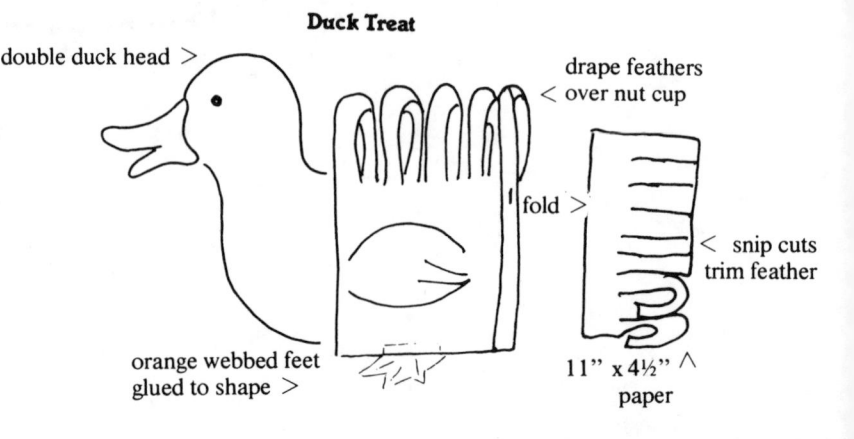

Duck Treat

- double duck head
- drape feathers over nut cup
- fold
- snip cuts trim feather
- orange webbed feet glued to shape
- 11" x 4½" paper

Egg Bouquet Centerpiece — Collect Styrofoam egg cartons of a variety of pastel shades. Cut out the individual egg cups. Vary the shape of cups by cutting edges so they have sharp corners, rounded corners, or deep narrow petals. Make stem with a colored pipe cleaner. Leaves made with crepe paper can be twisted around stem. Make arrangement by placing pipe cleaners in a pretty basket or bowl.

Egg Mobile — Twist together six pipe cleaners. Pull apart into a starburst form. At the end of each pipe cleaner attach an egg cup section. Hang the mobile by string from the light fixture or ceiling hook.

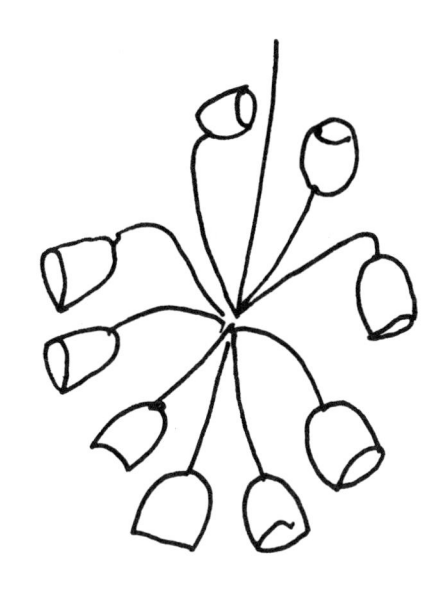

Menu and Recipes:

Baby Animal Sandwiches — Make animal shapes out of bread with cookie cutters. Fill with assorted meats and spreads. Use bits of pickle, cheese, pimento, or carrot for features.

Deviled Eggs

Carrot Raisin Salad

1 8¾ oz. can pineapple tidbits, drained
½ cup raisins

2 cups shredded carrots
mayonnaise to moisten

Mix pineapple, carrots, and raisins in a bowl and chill. Just before serving, add mayonnaise to moisten.

Spring Cooler

3 cups milk
1½ cups grape juice

whipped cream (in a can)
maraschino cherries

3 scoops vanilla ice cream

Combine milk, juice, and ice cream in blender until thick and foamy. Pour into glass and top with whipped cream and cherry.

Bunny Cake — Make favorite sheet cake and frost with a light blue or green frosting. Draw the outline of a bunny on the top and fill in outline using coconut. Use pink jelly beans for eyes and black licorice strings for whiskers.

Activities:

Hat Factory — Have assembled all sorts of materials that can be used to make hats. For hat bases have paper plate rims, construction paper cut into half circles for cone-shaped hats and paper bands. Also include all sorts of odds and ends such as doilies, paper flowers, or pipe cleaners, which can be used as decorations. After greetings invite guests to visit the table used as a hat factory and make their own special hat.

Spring Parade — Children wear new hats and march in a parade while an appropriate record is played. Award prizes for the prettiest, the funniest, the most unique, etc.

Rabbit Families — Choose two children to be rabbits. Each starts chasing other children. A child, when caught, joins hands with the rabbit who tagged him. They then run together and try to tag another player. The rabbit family with the largest number of members is the winner.

Jelly Bean Hunt — Prior to the party hide jelly beans of a variety of colors around the play area. Give each child a small basket or sack with one bean. The object of the game is to find and collect only beans that match the color of the one in the basket.

Peek and Guess — Cut vinyl wallpaper or soft leather into an egg shape. Cut windows of various sizes in the egg. Position behind the egg a picture of something familiar and easily recognized. Players peek in windows and speculate on what the big picture might be. The winner is the first one to guess correctly.

Sound Partner Hunt — Present to each child a picture of an animal that can be heard in the spring. Be sure another child has received an identical picture. Instruct children that, at the signal, they are the make the sound of their animal picture. Children crawl around the play area making that sound until they find another child making a similar sound. Older children can be blindfolded, but younger children will want to see where they're going.

Egg Hatching — Each child pretends to be a chick curled up inside an egg. Eyes are closed and there is very little movement. Slowly the chick begins to grow and can feel the sides of the shell pressing against wings and feet. To get out of the egg, the chick must peck a hole with beak and kick with feet. When the shell is broken, the chick takes its first steps and makes the first tiny sounds. Continue until the baby can run, fly, and flap wings.

Jelly Bean Spoon Race — Play like Rice Relay in the Japanese Party. At the end, divide jelly beans equally among guests.

Duck, Duck, Goose — Children sit in a circle. The child chosen to be "It" walks along the outside of the circle. When passing each child "It" taps his shoulder lightly and says, "Duck." After several tappings "It" then says, "Goose." At that clue the one tapped starts to chase "It" and tries to catch him before he reaches the empty space in the circle.

Goin' Fishin'

Goin' Fishin'

Ages: 4-8 years

Invitations:

Fishing Scene — Using construction paper draw, then cut out water, boats, fish, etc. The inside message of invitation can read something like, "John and his dad are going to a birthday fishing and field trip. Gather up your gear and come along on Saturday, June 12, at 10:00 a.m.!"

Decorations:

Nature Mobile — Make a form out of twigs. Hang from it mobile treasures found on the trip.

Painted Rocks — Collect interesting rocks. Paint a design on them then place on a basket or tray.

Nature Mobiles

twigs >

< nature treasures

Menu and Recipes:

Sandwiches — Favorites that are made with ingredients that won't make bread soggy.

Fruit — Firm fruit such as apples, oranges, or bananas.

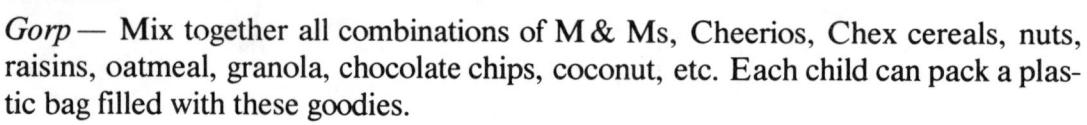

Gorp — Mix together all combinations of M & Ms, Cheerios, Chex cereals, nuts, raisins, oatmeal, granola, chocolate chips, coconut, etc. Each child can pack a plastic bag filled with these goodies.

Carrot Sticks

Surprise Cupcakes — Make Anna's Best Cake or your favorite recipe and fill cupcake papers ⅓ full, place several M & Ms or squares of chocolate or chocolate kisses in each paper. Fill each cake paper until it is ⅔ full. Bake and frost cupcakes as usual.

Cooler — Filled with water and canned drinks.

Activities:

Fishing — Every second of a fishing trip can be an adventure. Children will want to be included in the preparation of sandwiches and filling gorp bags. They will help dig or collect bait, can check condition of fishing gear, and help decide which places 'Old Fighter' might choose to hide. Some activities have been included to fill those midday hours when the fish are not biting, when the rain sends the troops to the tent, or there is an interesting nature area to explore near the fishing hole.

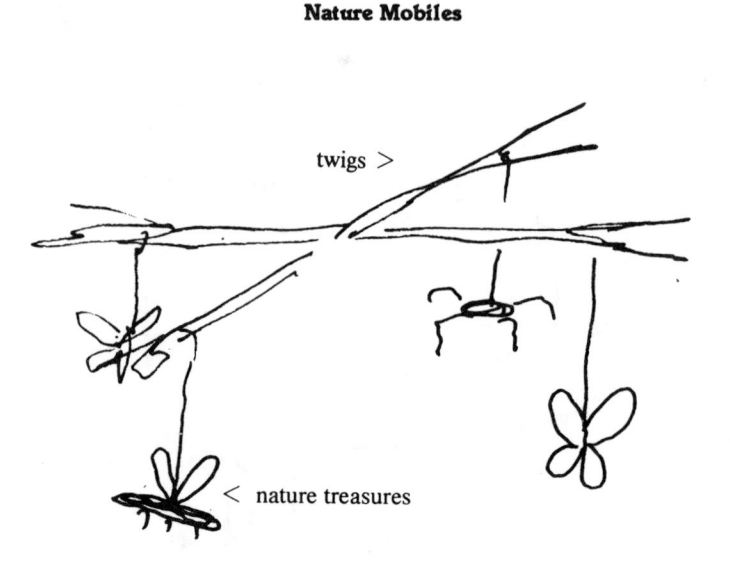

Adventure Hike — Divide the children into teams with half going with each adult. Set out in different directions to explore the "Wonders of Nature." When reunited share what was seen with exaggeration worthy of fisherman. For example: "I saw a mountain" (a hill), "We crossed a big river!" (a ditch) "We looked down into a big cave!" (a hole), "Before us was a gigantic waterfall!" (a small fall area in stream), "A piece of the moon!" (a rock), and so on.

Nature Scavenger Hunt — Prior to the trip make a list of specific types of nature objects to collect. If preferred the hunt can be a race. List could include: Bugs that jump, crawl, fly, or swim. Bugs that are fat, ugly, pretty, or with specific colors. Rocks that are flat, smooth, rough, tiny, shiny, round, etc. Seeds that have prickles, wings, are inside of fruit, etc.

Treasure Backpack — Cut a pillowcase in half, sew up raw opening on top piece. On bottom piece, turn top down ½ inch and hem. Attach a 2-foot-by-2-inch piece of material to each corner. Tie opposite string together in front. One pillowcase makes two backpacks.

Critter Cage — Cut "windows" out of sides of paper milk carton. Cut the foot off of a nylon stocking. Slip the stocking over the milk carton. Tie securely at the bottom. Leave the top loosely fastened so it can be easily opened when bugs are caught. Place a stick and leaves inside the cage so that the critter will feel at home.

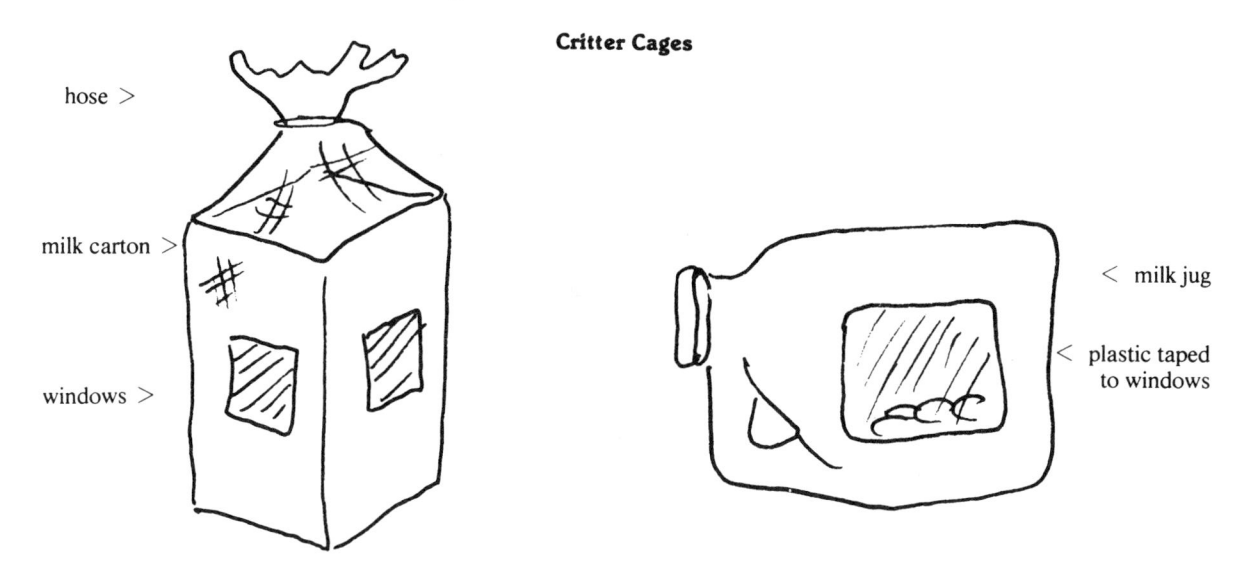

Critter Cages

hose >
milk carton >
windows >

< milk jug
< plastic taped to windows

What Do You See — While waiting for the fish to bite sharpen observational skills. What do you see jumping in the water, flying overhead, or standing on the distant hill? What kinds of shapes do you see in the clouds? At night, can you find the Milky Way, the Big Dipper, the moon or shooting stars?

In Case of Rain:

Feed Old Fighter — Cut a fish mouth in a plastic milk jug. Pretend it is Old Fighter. Feed this fish by trying to throw small rocks into his mouth. If several throws are successful move a greater distance from the target.

Fish Puzzles — Cut pictures of fish out of old outdoor magazines. Mount onto pieces of heavy paper. Cut each picture into several pieces. Place inside an envelope. Each child selects an envelope and tries to put puzzle quickly together.

Fishing Pond — Make a pond out of cardboard box. Use a stick, string, and magnet to make a fishing pole. Cut fish shapes out of construction paper. Attach a paper clip at mouth of each fish. To play, children take turns using the fishing pole. Try to catch fish all of one color, the biggest fish, or count the total number caught.

Hints:

Plan to have at least one other adult along. Take no more than four children.

Prior to the party scout the area thoroughly. Note the "wonders of nature" that can be pointed out to youngsters. Identify any potential hazards.

Contact the other adult who will go along on the fishing trip and parents of children to be invited. Agree on arrangements and have plans worked out before mentioning the party to children.

If adults are veterans at camping and fishing, the trip could be extended as an overnight camping expedition.

Check and double check all supplies and equipment. Include extra clothing and shoes, because children are sure to get wet!

Fish Puzzles

Fishing Pond

< stick
< string
< magnet
paper clip >
paper fish >

Water Carnival

Water Carnival

Ages: 6-9 years

Invitations:
Trace preceding picture and glue on a piece of folded construction paper. Write message inside. Make sure to remind children to wear bathing suits and bring a towel.

Decorations:
Balloons, crepe paper streamers, and paper lanterns on fences, trees, and carport.

Menu and Recipes:
Dunkin Dogs — Cut hots dogs into thirds and warm. Serve on a tray with toothpicks and dishes of catsup and mustard for dunkin'.

Watermelon — To be eaten later.

Splash Cake — Make sheet cake using recipe in Appendix or one of your own. Frost with medium blue frosting, then ripple the icing with spatula. Cut out a double form of cover picture and glue on popsicle stick. Place figure in center of cake. Add extra icing on top to make it look like the child has just jumped into the water.

Puddle Pies

1 cup flour	1 teaspoon salt
⅓ cup + 1 tablespoon shortening	2 tablespoons water

Mix ingredients together and roll into small balls. Mash each ball with your thumb. Bake at 350° for 10 minutes. Remove from oven and let cool. Fill with peanut butter.

Carnival Pudding

1 can (16 oz.) peach halves, well drained	1 box vanilla instant pudding mix
2 cups milk	3 tablespoons water
1 can coconut	red, yellow, and green food coloring

Tint coconut by placing 1 tablespoon water and 1 or 2 drops of food coloring in a small jar (a baby food jar is perfect). Add ¼ cup coconut, cover jar, and shake until coconut is evenly colored. Spread coconut out on a paper towel and allow to dry a few minutes. Repeat procedure for each color wanted. Mix pudding according to package directions and allow to cool. To serve, place drained peach half on a lettuce leaf and fill center with pudding. Garnish by sprinkling with tinted coconut just before serving.

Activities:

Arrival — Enjoy splashing in pool or playing in a tub of water. Have plenty of water toys available.

Seed pitching — Give each child 20 watermelon seeds when he arrives. Use string to denote a line about 1 yard from the wall. Children take turns pitching seeds against the wall, trying to get them to land close to it. Each player pitches one seed, which must bounce off of the wall, for each round. The child whose seed is closest to the wall gets all of the seeds pitched that round. The game can continue until one child has all of the seeds or the children tire of the game.

Water Balloon Bungle — Make rackets for each child from coat hangers bent into an oval shape and covered with a piece of nylon hose. For safety be sure to cover tip of handle with masking tape (see illustration). Fill ten balloons with water. When ready to play game, divide the children into two teams and give the leader of each team five balloons. At the signal, the first child walks to the balloons and picks up a balloon on his racket without using his hands. He then walks to the next person in line and transfers the balloon to his racket without touching it. This person turns to the next child and repeats the process until the last child places the balloon on the ground without his hands. As the first balloon is traveling through the line, the first child starts a second, a third, etc. The team to get the most balloons moved through the line without being broken is the winner.

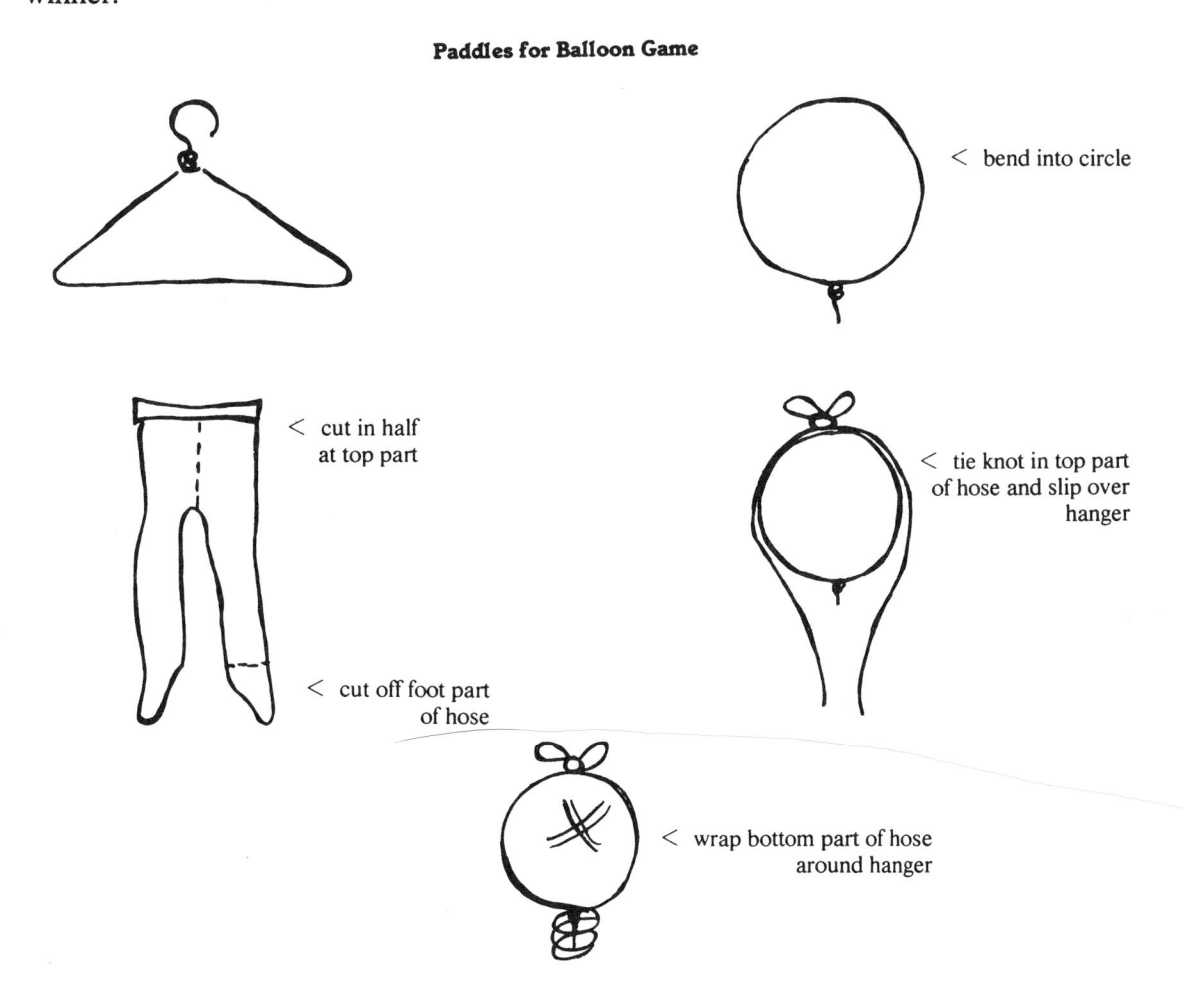

Paddles for Balloon Game

< bend into circle

< cut in half at top part

< tie knot in top part of hose and slip over hanger

< cut off foot part of hose

< wrap bottom part of hose around hanger

137

Jump the Stream — Children form a circle with an adult holding a water hose in the center. The leader gives a signal to begin and starts turning slowly keeping the stream of water close to the ground. As the water gets close to a child, he has to jump to avoid getting wet. Each time the adult completes a full revolution, he begins to turn a little faster and raises the stream slightly off of the ground. When children are squirted, they leave the circle and the other children step inward to fill his place. The game continues until only one child is left.

Wadmitton — Use rackets used in the Water Balloon Bungle and make a paper ball for each player. Define the playing court with a net as high as the children's heads. Divide the children into two groups and place them on opposite sides of the net. When the leader says "go," all players hit their paper wads over the net. When a wad comes over the net, it is hit back. When a wad hits the ground, it can no longer be in play. There is no limit on the number of times a wad can be hit before it touches the ground. The game continues until all wads have landed on the ground. They are then counted and the team with the least number of wads on its side wins.

Seed Spittin' — All children are given a large slice of watermelon. At the signal, they begin to eat their portion, stopping to spit their seeds as they eat. The child who is able to propel a seed the longest distance from where he is sitting is the winner.

School Daze

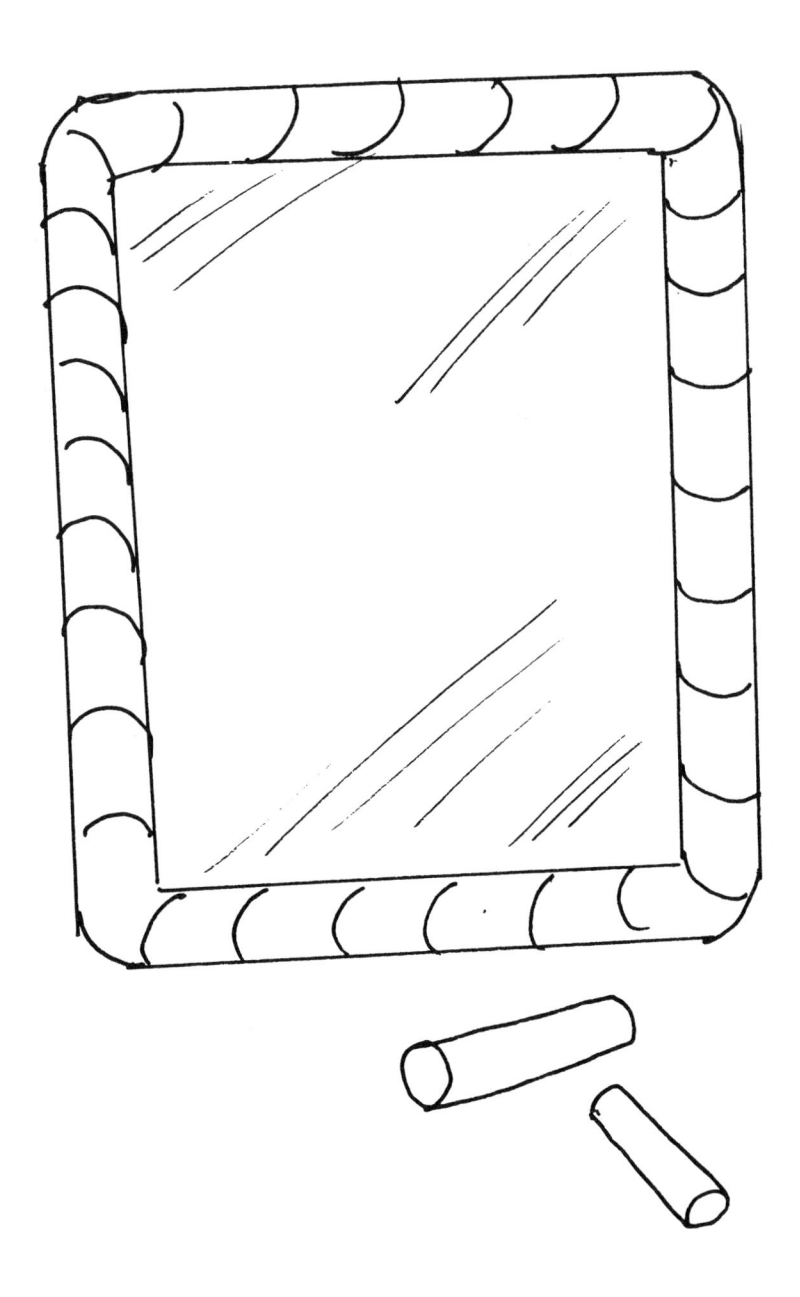

School Daze Birthday

Ages: 5-8 years

Invitations:

Cut 4-by-6-inch rectangles out of black construction paper, rounding the corners. Next cut a ¾-inch frame for the rectangle out of light brown paper and glue to the black rectangle. Lace a border around the brown border using black yarn or string. Write invitation using chalk or a white grease pencil (see illustration).

Decorations:

Mobile — Made with leaves cut from fall shades of construction paper and tied onto branches

Math-o-Mats — Make large slates with 8½-by-11-inch brown paper. Write several math problems on each one. The children can try to solve them while they are waiting for the food.

Centerpiece — Schoolhouse: Cover a ½-gallon milk carton with construction paper. Add windows and doors. Make play equipment out of popsicle sticks, or toothpicks. A small box can be decorated to look like a bus.

Favors — A pencil, eraser, and small tablets for each guest.

Menu and Recipes:

Sack lunches in shoe boxes or paper bags decorated by the guests when they arrive. Each lunch should contain: a sandwich, an apple or small box of raisins, and several alphabet crackers. Mix 1 cup finely shredded cheese with ½ teaspoon minced onion and enough mayonnaise to make a stiff paste. Place mixture in a decorator bag and use #16, #17, or #32 tip. Write a letter on each saltine square.

OR

Alphabet Soup — Served in cups.

Namewiches — Place a slice of ham on a piece of bread and cut into four squares. Soften 3 oz. of cream cheese and mix with ½ to 1 teaspoon mustard. Place mixture in a decorating bag and write a letter on each square using a #2 or #3 plain round tip. Children choose squares which, when placed together, will spell their name.

Fruit Fluff — Slice one banana and chop one apple. Mix together with a 1 lb. can of fruit cocktail, well drained, and one 4 oz. container of frozen whipped topping.

Brownie Cake

8 eggs
2 bars sweet cooking chocolate (melted and cooled)
1 cup Bisquick baking mix
1 cup granulated sugar
1 cup packed brown sugar
1½ cup chopped nuts (optional)
½ cup softened butter or margarine

Heat oven to 350°. Grease 9-by-13-inch cake pan. Beat all ingredients except nuts until smooth (approximately 2 minutes if a mixer is used). Pour into pan. Sprinkle with nuts or use M & Ms to spell out Happy Birthday (child's name). Bake 30 to 35 minutes (until knife comes out clean). If M & Ms are not used for message, use an aerosol canned whipped topping to write it.

Activities:

Rotten Apple — Cut 14 apples out of red construction paper and one apple out of brown paper. Color the stem and leaves with a green magic marker. Mount apples on a piece of heavy white construction paper. Recut the apple shapes. To play, invite children to sit in a circle. Place all of the apples face down in a basket. Each child takes a turn picking an apple out of the basket. The one who gets the brown apple is eliminated. The apples are then mixed up and returned to the basket. The game continues until only one child remains.

< fill blanks with S T E M

fill blanks with L E A F >

< apple cards

< fill blanks with A P P L E

Secrets — Hang several sheets of large newsprint on the wall or use a blackboard. Divide the children into two groups that form two lines in front of the paper or blackboard. The child nearest the paper or blackboard is given a pencil or chalk and instructed to draw the same picture on the blackboard or paper that the person behind him drew on his back. The child at the end of each line begins the game by drawing a picture, shape, etc., with his finger on the back of the person in front of him. That person then draws the same picture on the back in front of him. Continue until the child with marker draws the picture. This picture is then compared to the original. The game continues until each child has had a turn to both begin a picture and draw it in its final stage.

Word Scramble (older children) — Use the letters in Happy Birthday and Birthday Child's name. Children write as many words as they can think of in 10 minutes.

Baked Apple — Children sit in a circle and pass either a plastic apple or small ball around the circle as music is played. When the music stops, the person holding the apple is out. Continue playing until only one child is remaining.

Apple Scramble — Divide the playing area into two equal parts with a center line that is clearly marked. Next, divide the children into two groups and put each group on opposite sides of the center line. Place 5 to 7 Nerf, tennis, or playground balls on the center line. On command, the children run to get as many balls as possible to throw to the other side. Children must throw balls as quickly as possible. The game continues for about 1 minute with an adult counting down the last 10 seconds. No balls may be thrown at the end of the count. Count the "apples" on each side. The side with the least number is considered to have the quickest throwers. Hint: Maintain safety standards by watching to see that children throw the balls only toward the ground, not at each other.

Spin the Worm — Prepare game board with spinner and enough apple word cards for each player as illustrated. Children take turns spinning the worm. Write in the appropriate space on apple the letter pointed to by worm spinner. If the letter is already filled the player must wait until the next round before spinning again. Continue until someone wins by filling in all the space.

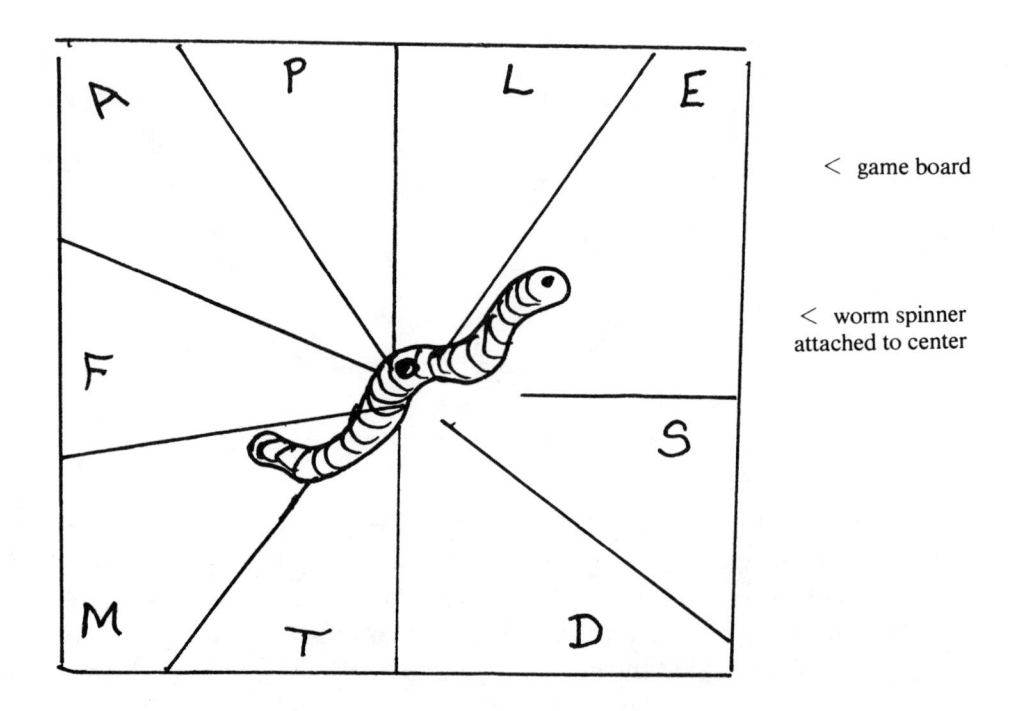

< game board

< worm spinner attached to center

Halloween Happening

Halloween Happening

Ages: 5-8 years

Invitations:

Duplicate illustration of a haunted house. Make a ghost with white construction paper. Write message on ghost before attaching, as shown, above the window with a strip of accordian folded paper.

Decorations:

Spiders — Make bodies with egg carton cups. Use pipe cleaners as legs. Suspend from white yarn webs.

Paper Witches, Jack-o'-Lanterns, Black Cats, Ghosts, Skeletons, Bats — Can be attached to ends of twisted black and orange crepe paper streamers.

Haunted House — Enlarge pattern and draw on a large piece of butcher paper. Attach to a wall.

OR

Decorate a large box to look like a haunted house. Invite children to crawl into the dark creep house to search for hidden prizes. (Dangle creepy things from string or tape from the top and sides of the box).

Ghost Straws and Spider Name Cards — Make ghost shapes out of white construction paper, add black eyes and mouth, and put on the table. Cut two slits and slip ghosts over the straws.

Goblin Mats — Cut unusual shapes out of green construction paper and draw scary faces on them.

Centerpiece — A haunted house cake surrounded with Halloween candy objects.

Menu and Recipes:

Ghost Sandwiches — Thickly spread a piece of bread with peanut butter and cut bread in half. Cut a banana in half lengthwise and crosswise. Place 2 quarters on each half of bread and add 2 raisins for eyes.

Molded Monster Fingers — Make lime gelatin according to package directions. Allow to cool until thick. Add 2 cups of shredded carrots and ½ cup pineapple. Chill until set. Slice in 2-by-4-inch strips. Serve on lettuce leaf, garnished with a "whipped cream fingernail."

Pumpkin Cups — Cut off cap from orange and remove pulp. Draw a face on outside using a black magic marker or black construction paper cut-outs glued to the surface. Fill with fruit and replace cap. Stick a toothpick in the cap to be used later when eating the fruit.

Green Ghoul — Place 10 to 15 butterscotch chips in each mug. Add milk that has been heated until it steams. Add a few drops of green food coloring and several miniature marshmallows. Stir and serve.

Haunted House Cake — Make a sheet cake and frost it with orange frosting. Draw outlines for haunted house on it and ice the house with chocolate frosting. Add finishing touches using vanilla wafers, graham crackers, flat chocolate bars, candy corn and Halloween candy (see illustration).

Frozen Jack-o'-Lanterns

1 8 oz. box plain yogurt   16 oz. container frozen, unsweetened orange juice

Mix well and freeze in a cupcake pan before serving. Draw Jack-o'-Lantern faces in ice cream with chocolate frosting.

Activities:

Spooky Pictures — Soon after children arrive, they may draw a scary picture on black paper with black wax crayons. (Add atmosphere by playing spooky mood music). When drawing is complete, brush over entire picture with white tempera paint that has been thinned with water. After party, pictures can be taken home.

Haunted Hunt — Prior to party, draw or cut from books or magazine, three pictures of Halloween scenes. Back with construction paper, then cut pictures into three or four puzzle pieces. Keep one key piece of each puzzle and hide the remaining parts around the party area. Divide the guests into three teams. Give each team one puzzle piece. Each team tries to find the rest of their puzzle within a designated time limit.

Feel the Ghosts — Hide a variety of small objects (comb, keys, eraser, flashbulb, plastic spoon, tiny car, etc.) in a white sock that has been decorated with two large button eyes. Tie a string around the opening of sock. Pass the sock around and allot each child about one minute to identify the objects in the sock by touching. Without telling anyone else, each child writes guesses of objects on a slip of paper. Award a prize to the one with the best answers. Hint: If children are younger, provide each with one sock that contains a single item. The child feels sock and guesses contents before opening the sock. He then keeps the prize in the sock!

Spiders and Flies — The child chosen to be the spider stands inside a web (a rope circle). Other children pretend to be flies. They buzz as near to the spider as possible but try not to get caught. If the spider tags a fly, he then joins the spider inside the web. Continue game until most of the flies are caught.

Haunted House Bingo — Make Haunted House game boards, each with 25 spaces. Place game pieces (cat, ghost, goblin, skeleton, etc.) randomly on the boards. Draw or clip from magazines or books pictures to match words. Print word and paste picture on a 3-by-5-inch card. To play the game, place all picture cards in a bowl and provide each player with a Haunted House gameboard and markers. Draw a picture card from the bowl. All players with that picture name will cover space or spaces with a marker. Place card back in box and draw again. Continue playing until someone covers five spaces in a horizontal, vertical, or diagonal row.

Haunted House Variation — If children are younger, make Haunted House gameboards with nine spaces. Draw a ghost for each space and draw or paste on the ghost a Halloween character. Make identical ghost cards and place in drawing bowl. To play the game, a child picks a ghost card from the bowl. If a match is made, place ghost card over the appropriate ghost space. If no match is possible, throw the card back into the drawing bowl. Children take turns until someone fills all the spaces on the drawing card.

Tip the Ghosts — Decorate plastic milk cartons to look like ghosts. Set in a row on a ledge or table. To play, the child stands about five feet away and tries to knock over ghosts with a bean bag or Nerf ball.

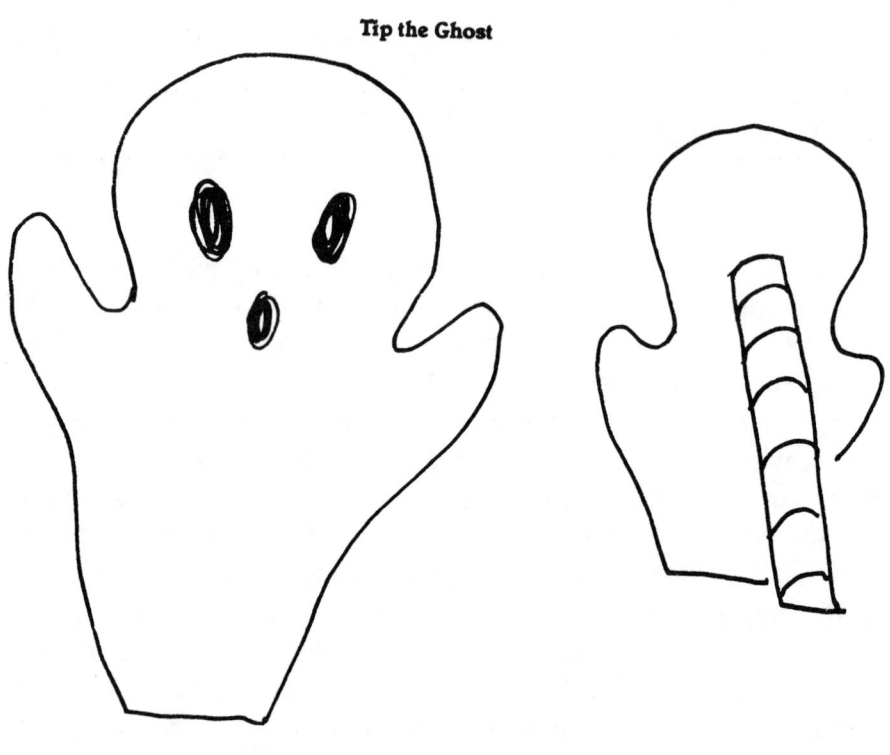

Tip the Ghost

Pin the Tail on the Devil (Another "Donkey" Variation) — Draw a picture of devil onto a large piece of construction paper or posterboard, color it, and place an X where the tail would be. Make tails out of black construction paper. Put a piece of tape at the top of the tail on the backside. Children take turns and are given a tail, blindfolded, then turned around in a circle three times. They then try to walk over and pin the tail over the X.

The Goblins Are Coming — Children divide into sets of two and determine what Halloween characters they will represent. Use a piece of masking tape, a plastic ring or a rope to identify the "home" of each character. The couple designated as goblins do not have "homes." The game begins with goblins walking slowly around the play area. Whenever they call out the Halloween name of a team, that team leaves "home" and starts walking. To get everyone out of their "home" the goblins say, "The night is calm." When the goblins call, "The goblins are coming!" all run to a home as quickly as possible. The couple left without a home will become the new goblins.

Harvest Birthday Gathering

Harvest Birthday Gathering

Ages: 5-9 years

Invitations:

Cut out a double scarecrow with a fold on head. Decorate the front using crayons, yarn, pieces of cloth scraps, and straw. In the message suggest that guests come dressed to look like scarecrows.

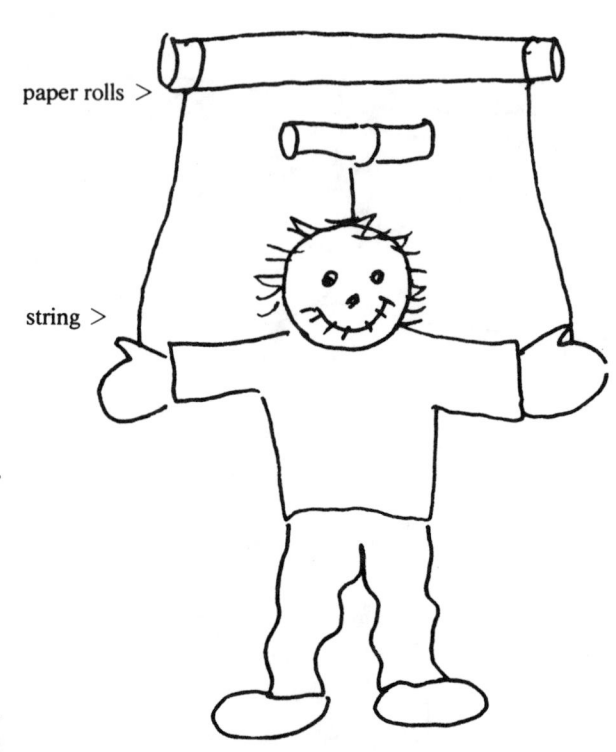

Decorations:

Scarecrow Puppet — Cut head, body, gloves, and shoes out of poster board. Use crepe paper or strips of cloth for arms and legs. Glue or staple parts together. Decorate the scarecrows using yarn, straw, strips of paper for hair, buttons for eyes, and odds and ends of wallpaper, foil, and cloth for clothes. Tie a string from the head to a cardboard tube and from hands to another cardboard tube. When puppets are not dancing they can be hanging as decorations for party area.

Room — Arrange yellow, orange, red, and brown paper chains or crepe paper streamers around room.

Table — Cover table with tan or brown paper. Leaf placemats can be made by first gathering pretty fall leaves. Place leaves carefully on a 12-by-18-inch piece of wax paper. On top of the arrangement place another piece of wax paper of identical size. Cover with a cloth or paper so the iron won't stick to the wax paper. Iron wax paper sheets together. A colorful border of construction paper can be added if desired.

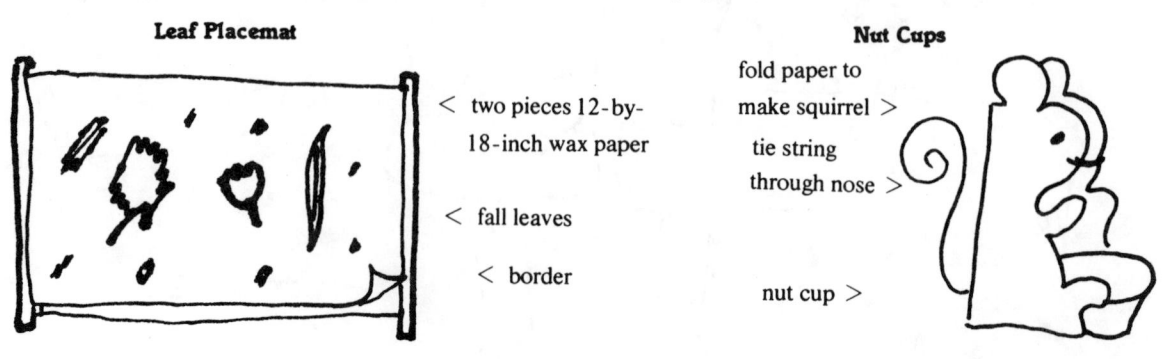

Nut Cups — Cut a half squirrel shape. Punch a tiny hole in nose. Tie nose pieces around a nut cup. Complete by adding a tail made with a fuzzy brown pipe cleaner or construction paper that has been fringed on edges. Fill nut cups with candy corn, nuts, and mints.

Black Crow Name Cards — Each crow requires two black construction paper cylinders. The one for the head is half the size of the body. Fasten head and body cylinders together with paper fasteners or tiny stapler. Cut a black construction paper rectangle the size of the body for wing tips. Glue wings and tail to body. Add beak, eyes, and feet. Write the names of guests on strips of white paper and glue to wings.

Centerpiece — Create a colorful fall arrangement with harvest foods such as squash, pumpkins, nuts, and apples.

Scarecrow Name Tag

Menu and Recipes:

Scarecrow Sandwiches — Cut brown bread with gingerbread-shaped cookie cutter. Fill as desired.

Celery, Apple, and Raisin Salad

Apple Cider

Scarecrow Cake — Bake two gingerbread mixes in two rectangular pans. Cut pieces as illustrated. Mix icing, then divide into three parts before adding tints. Ice each part, then attach (the icing acts as glue). Complete features using candy corn, raisins, M & Ms, gold licorice, and nuts.

Scarecrow Cake

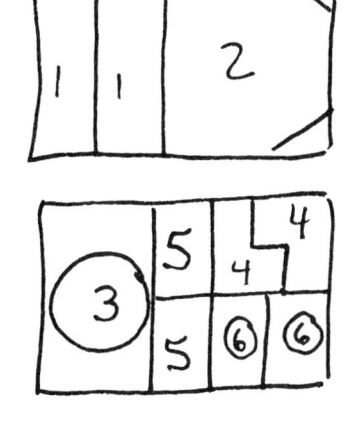

1. legs
2. body
3. head
4. boots
5. arms
6. gloves
7. cardboard hat

Activities:

Scarecrow Action Poem — Follow directions in the poem.
> Scarecrow, scarecrow, turn around.
> Scarecrow, scarecrow, jump up and down.
> Scarecrow, scarecrow, arms up high.
> Scarecrow, scarecrow, touch the sky.
> Scarecrow, scarecrow, bend your knees.
> Scarecrow, scarecrow, flop in the breeze.
> Scarecrow, scarecrow, wink one eye.
> Scarecrow, scarecrow, say "goodbye."

Gather the Nuts — Before the party hide different nuts in shells around the party area. Provide each child with a small paper bag. At the signal they all try to gather as many nuts as possible.

How Many Kernels? — Count the number of kernels of corn needed to fill a jar. During the party guests estimate the number contained. Be sure to write their guesses on a piece of paper. The winner is the one who guessed nearest to the correct answer.

Scarecrow Tag — The child designated as the scarecrow is "glued" to an assigned spot. In pockets and on floor near scarecrow are paper ears of corn. Other children pretend to be crows. They try to steal the corn without being tagged by the scarecrow.

Hot Potato — Children group into two teams. Designate an area for each team, with a rope in between. Provide each player with a Nerf ball or sponge. At the signal, "Hot Potato," the balls become too hot to hold. The children keep throwing the balls until signaled to stop. The winning team is the group with the least number of potatoes.

Hide the Walnuts — Children close eyes or go out of the room while one child hides a walnut. He then guides the others in the search by calling, "warm," "cold," or "hot," according to the distance away from the nut. A variation of this game is to have the child go out of the room while others observe where the nut is hidden. As child searches for the nut he is directed by soft to loud volume of hums by the other children.

Squirrels and Trees — Form several trees by pairs of children clasping hands together. Each tree is the home for another child, who is a squirrel. Outside tree arms one child is a squirrel without a home. At the signal, "Run squirrels! Run!" the trees lift limbs (arms) and squirrels scamper to find a new home. The squirrel without a home tries to be one of the fortunate squirrels. After a few runs, have the squirrel players and one half of the tree players change positons. Continue to play the game. Change squirrels with the other half of tree players before finishing the game.

Toyland Birthday

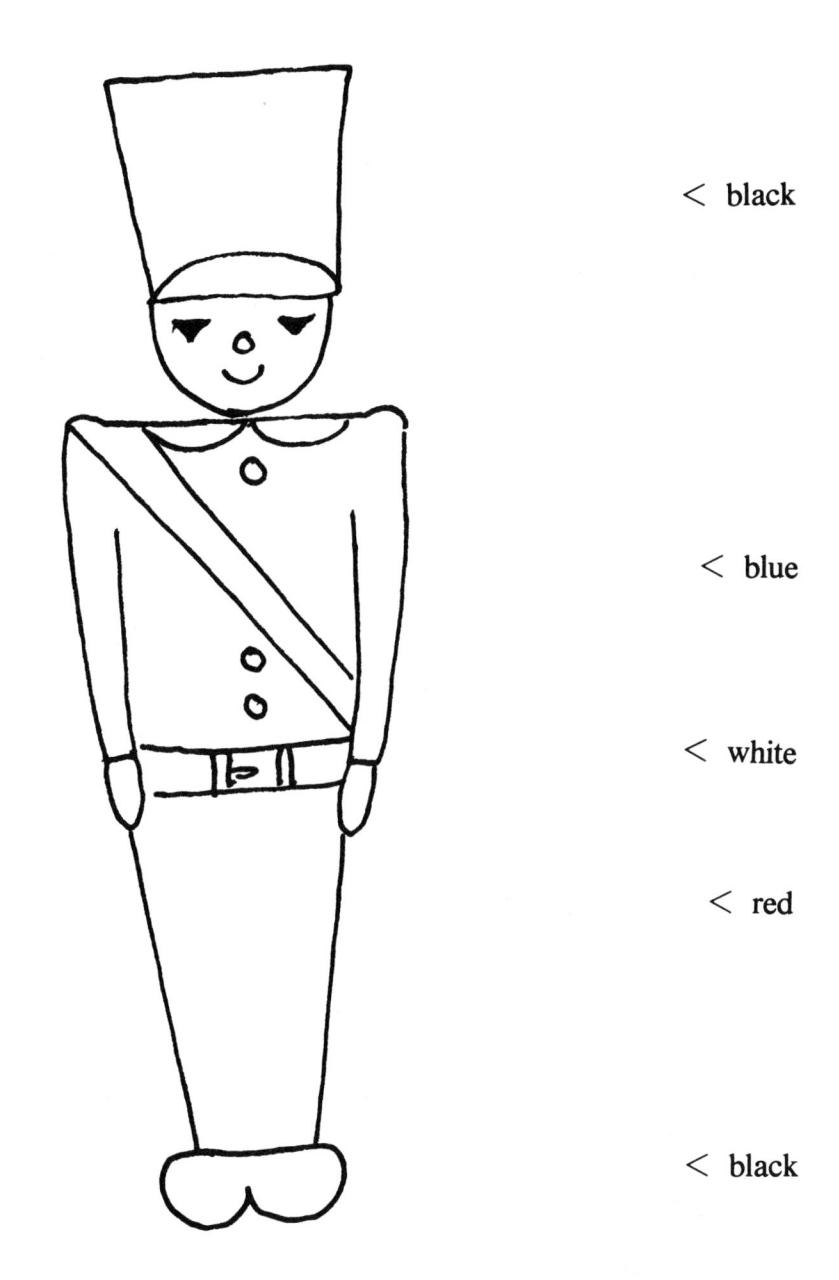

< black

< blue

< white

< red

< black

Cut two – paste colored parts of uniform on soldier with party information on back.

Toyland Birthday

Ages: 3-5 years

Invitations:
Toy Soldier doubled with front decorated and message on inside. (See illustration.)

Decorations:

Candy Canes — Paint wrapping paper cardboard tubes white. Make stripes with red crepe paper. If desired, a bow can be placed on each.

Toy Trains — Decorate cardboard boxes to look like cars of a train. Place in each box toys children may wish to play with when they tire of organized games.

Toy Box

Toy Mobile — Cut pictures of toys from catalogs or magazines. Mount on construction paper. Hang from light fixture or ceiling hook and attach the toy pictures with string.

Table — Place white tablecloth on table. Have red crepe paper strips diagonally crossing at the center of the table. Use white plates with colorful napkins cut out in a shape of a toy vehicle placed on plate.

Place Cards

< glue on drum stick separately

Place Cards — Make place cards by folding paper to resemble a drum. The name of the child is placed on a paper drum stick.

Centerpiece — Create a toy castle with a shoe box, spools, and cardboard cylinders. (At the end of the party open toy castle to find special toy favors for each child). Toy soldiers surrounding the castle can be made with clothespins or paper cylinders.

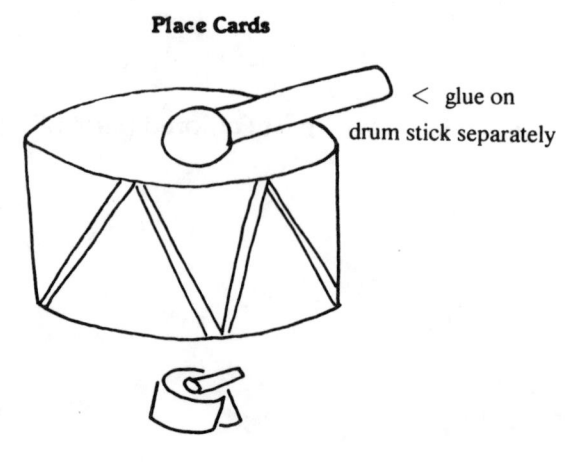

Menu and Recipes:

Gingerbread Men — Prepare dough ahead of time. At the party roll dough so that each child may cut out and then decorate his gingerbread man with raisins, cinnamon, or candies. Bake according to directions.

Peppermint Flip — Place one scoop of peppermint ice cream into a glass. Fill with ginger ale. Place a small candy cane over the rim of each glass.

Candied Apples — Use pre-made candied apple wrappers, your own recipe, or the recipe on the back of the caramel bag.

Gingerbread House Birthday Cake — Bake favorite cake in two 8-inch square pans. Cover with white icing. Using cake decorating kit, mints, and candy canes, make windows, doors, and a roof.

Activities:

Toy Soldier March — Make soldier costumes by using white crepe paper strips that crisscross on front of the child and are stapled in back at waist level. As "March of the Toy Soldiers" or another record is played, children march around the room. Keep knees and arms stiff and head looking straight ahead. Older children may enjoy variations of obeying orders, such as "march forward," "step backward," "turn to left," or "turn around."

Button Toys — Collect buttons, carpet string, and a paper cup.

1) Thread carpet string through two holes of a large button. Tie ends. Twirl the string until it is quite tight. Pull back and forth so toy makes a whizzing sound.

2) Punch a hole through the bottom of a paper cup. Thread carpet string through a large button, then knot at the end. Pull the string through hole, then tie a knot in the cup. The object of the game is to swing cup and catch the button.

Button Toy

Jack-in-the-Box — Dramatize
  Jack-in-the-Box sits so still.
  (Children squat with heads down).
  Won't you come out?
  Yes I will!
  (Children pop up).

< carpet thread

Teddy Bear Game — Dramatize the following:
  Teddy Bear, Teddy Bear, show your shoe.
  Teddy Bear, Teddy Bear, that will do.
  Teddy Bear, Teddy Bear, turn around.
  Teddy Bear, Teddy Bear, touch the ground.
  Teddy Bear, Teddy Bear, go upstairs.
  Teddy Bear, Teddy Bear, say your prayers.
  Teddy Bear, Teddy Bear, switch off the lights.
  Teddy Bear, Teddy Bear, say "goodnight."

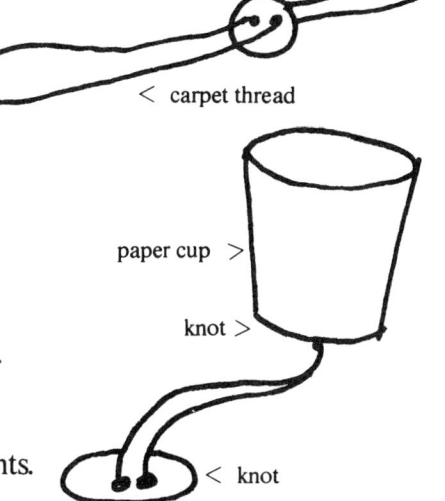

paper cup >

knot >

< knot

Toy Factory — Say "It's time to see if the toys in the factory work properly so they can be sent to boys and girls." As name of toy is called, children dramatize the action. Examples: airplane flies, balls bounce, tops twirl, dolls say "Ma-Ma." Toys that don't work are sent back to the factory.

Toy Train — Children may play with toys placed in the cardboard train boxes or take out the toys and play with the boxes.

Appendix

Recipes and Decorating Instructions

On demand from friends, one of the authors' favorite recipes is included. The birthday cakes described in this book can be made using Anna's recipe, your favorite recipe, or a packaged cake mix.

Anna's Best Cake

¾ cup shortening
1½ teaspoon vanilla
3¾ cups cake flour
3¾ teaspoon baking powder
2¼ cups sugar
3 eggs
½ cup powdered milk
1½ teaspoon salt
1½ cups plus 1 tablespoon water

Cream shortening and sugar until light (12 to 15 minutes) using medium high speed on an electric mixer. Add vanilla and eggs one at a time. Mix well after each egg. Sift cake flour, powdered milk, baking powder and salt. Add to creamed mixture alternately with water. Beat after each addition. Hint: There is less mess if water is added first. Bake in a 9-by-13-inch cake pan at 375° until done (approximately 30 to 40 minutes).

OR

For chocolate cake, add ¾ cup powdered cocoa, ¼ cup butter or margarine, or 4 squares melted unsweetened chocolate. Add margarine or chocolate with shortening and cocoa with dry ingredients.

Tips for Better Baking

Even the prettiest decorations cannot improve the appearance of a lopsided cake. Follow these instructions for the best results:

Preheat the oven before baking the cake.

Line the bottom of the cake pan with a piece of wax paper that has been cut to fit the pan.

Just before placing the filled pans in the oven for baking, tap them on the edge of the countertop four times. After each tap, turn the pan a quarter turn. This will help remove the air bubbles and produce a finer textured cake. If the cake appears to have more air bubbles, repeat this procedure until most of them have disappeared.

While cake is baking, do not open the oven door to check on the cake's progress until it has been baking for at least 20 to 25 minutes.

Check the cake for doneness by inserting a toothpick in the middle of cake. *If the removed toothpick is clean, the cake is finished.*

Allow the cake to cool inside the pan for 5 to 10 minutes. Run a table knife along the inside of the pan to loosen the sides of the cake. Place a wire rack over the top of the pan. Invert the rack and pan together. Remove the pan and lift off the wax paper.

Brush off all loose crumbs from the top and sides of the cake and let it cool for at least 1 hour before freezing or icing.

For best results, wrap a cake in foil or put it in a plastic bag before freezing.

Bake the cake ahead and freeze it. This will help to prevent a crumbly cake surface. It will also save time as the party day draws near.

Icing the Cake

No Fail Frosting

1½ lb. 10 X powdered sugar (sift if lumpy)   ¾ teaspoon salt
1 teaspoon cream of tartar   ½ cup Crisco (no substitutes)
½ cup of water (do not add all at once)   1½ teaspon flavoring (almond is preferred)

Place dry ingredients, Crisco and flavoring in a bowl. Add the water as needed to make the icing a medium consistency. Beat for approximately five minutes. Frosting will keep for several days if the bowl of frosting is covered with plastic wrap or cloth and placed in the refrigerator.

Place cake on the platter to be used for serving. (A very inexpensive cake platter can be made by covering a cardboard case for canned sodas with aluminum foil). If cake is a little lopsided or the top is bumpy, trim and level with a sharp knife.

Remove ¾ cup of frosting from the bowl. Add approximately ¾ cups of warm water to the frosting and mix well. This is called a crumb coating mixture. It reduces the amount of crumbs left on the cake surface and acts as a seal to prevent drying. Spread the mixture over the sides of the cake first. Make sure to seal the area between the cake side and platter. Complete by covering the top. If two layers of cake are used an alternate type of filling can be placed between the layers. One suggestion is to use your favorite jam or jelly.

Allow the crumb coating to dry for at least five hours before adding the remainder of icing to the cake. Take the bowl of icing out of refrigerator. Soften it by mixing 1 minute at medium speed with an electric mixer. Choose the tints that will be now added. A general rule for use is to make the background a lighter tint and the detailed decorations with deeper, more vivid colors. Add tint to icing sparingly until the desired color is obtained.

Use a short metal spatula to ice cake. Start on sides by stroking from top to bottom so that any loose crumbs that mght be on the cake surface are pushed to the base. Be sure to seal the area between the cake and the platter. Add the remaining icing to the top of the cake.

Use a short metal spatula to smooth the icing on the sides of the cake. To do this, dip the spatula in hot water, then wipe dry with a paper towel. Press the warm spatula gently against the sides of the cake. Apply even pressure while pulling the cake toward you. Wipe the excess icing off the spatula and repeat the procedure on the next side. Continue until all sides are smooth. Smooth the top by using a long metal spatula, which is dipped in warm water and wiped dry as necessary. Smooth icing by making sweeping strokes from side to side. If the first attempt is not successful the entire procedure can be repeated.

Allow the layer of icing to dry for at least two hours so that the top will form a crust. A logical time schedule is to bake, crumb coat, and ice the cake one day and decorate it the next. An uncut cake carefully sealed with the crumb coating mixture and icing will stay fresh for up to 6 days.

Decorating the Cake

Decorator's Perfect Icing
1 egg white   1¼ cups Crisco
1½ lb. 10X powdered sugar (sift for lumps)
1½ teaspoon flavoring (almond is recommended)
Place all ingredients in a bowl and beat for 10 to 15 minutes at low speed with an electric mixer. Divide icing according to the number of tints and approximate amount of each needed to decorate the cake. If you plan to use one color in several areas, mix enough of it in the beginning as it is difficult to duplicate tints exactly.

Illustration Transfer

Trace the pattern illustrations from this book onto a piece of wax paper. Position the wax paper on the top of cake and trace the lines with a toothpick or other pointed object. Press hard enough so that the pattern is visible on the icing.

Decorating Bag — Preparation and Use

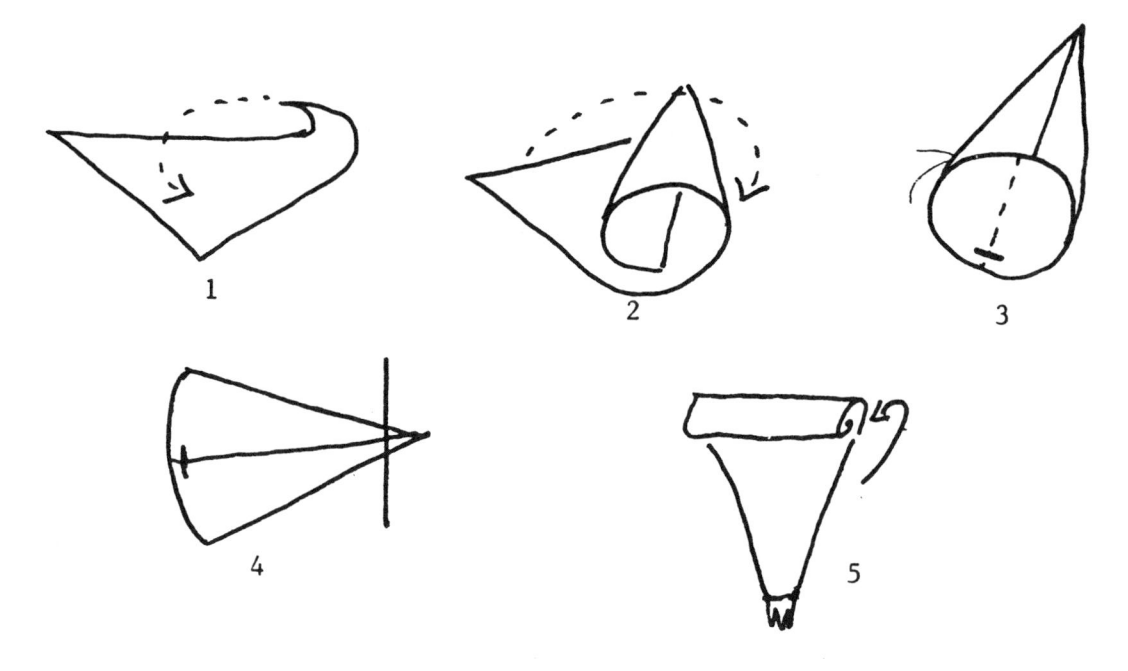

If bags have not been purchased, they can easily be made with parchment or wax paper. Cut a 12-inch square of paper. Fold opposite corners together to form a triangle. Lay the triangular piece of paper flat with the right hand. Fold this corner up and over to the center. Make a cone shape by holding these two points together and rolling the point on the left side until it meets the other two points. Secure by folding point down once, then stapling or making two tears in the fold and folding this smaller piece once more. Cut approximately ¾ inches off the tip of the cone.

Standard decorating tips are a medium star tip for filling in patterns, the large opening star tip used for borders and the small opening plain round tip for writing and adding finishing touches to patterns. It saves time when decorating to have several tips available. A recommended number is four #16 or #17 small opening star tips, two #34 large opening star tips, and three #2 or #3 small opening writing tips. If the number available is limited it will be necessary to wash tips each time colors are changed.

Drop the appropriate tip into the bag. Make sure the small tip protrudes enough so that the paper is above the tip opening. Hold the bag at opening. Use a small metal spatula to fill the bag ½ full and push icing down into the bag. Keep folding the seam side of the bag while tucking the excess paper inside this fold until the bag tightly encloses the icing. Pick up the decorating bag at the larger fold with your writing hand and hold the small end of the bag with the other. Air bubbles are prevented by continuing a steady pressure with both hands.

Types of Decorations

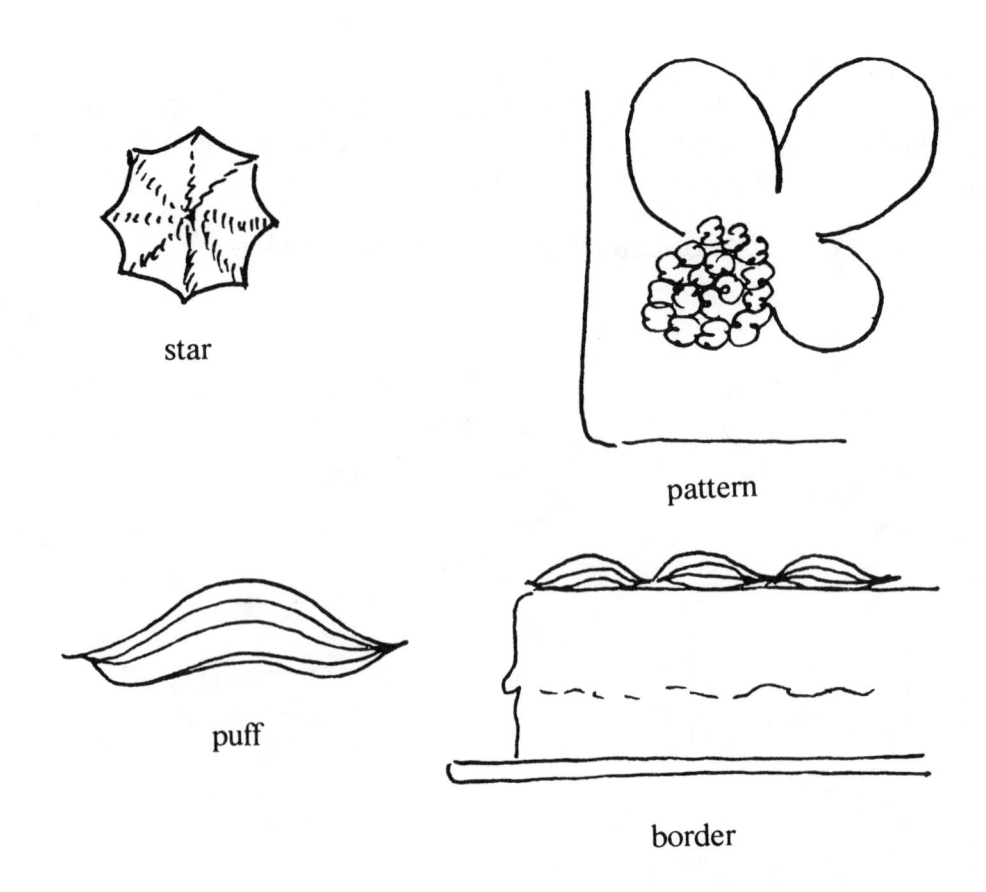

star

pattern

puff

border

Stars – Used to fill in picture outlines. Hold bag at 90 degree angle with the tip of the tube almost touching the surface of the decorating area. Squeeze the bag to form a star. Stop squeezing and pull the tube away. Continue, arranging individual stars side by side until the picture outline is complete.

Puffs – Used to make borders around the top and bottom edge of cake. Hold decorating bag at a 45 degree angle with the end of the bag facing toward you. Touch the tube to the surface. Apply a light-heavy-light pressure as the icing is squeezed out of the bag. The puff ends when all pressure has stopped. Be sure to make minor adjustments near the end of the last side to be decorated so that there is uniformity in puff size.

Hint – If right handed, start decorating the cake in the upper left hand corner and work in counterclockwise direction. Reverse direction if left handed. Slowly turn the cake while decorating so that the working side is always nearest.

Writing – Fill the bag with the thinner consistency of icing. Hold the bag at a 45-degree angle with the wide end pointing toward you. Touch the tube lightly to the surface and squeeze so that icing sticks. Lift the tube slightly and move it in a straight line down. Stop the pressure and pull the tube away at the end of the stroke. Practice straight, curved, and slanted lines and then combine these strokes to form different letters. Hint: Try to use your whole arm, not just fingers. The arm movement is very important in completing satisfactory and professional looking letters.

Before actually decorating the cake, plan to practice each type of decoration on the back of a cake pan. When the cake pan is full, or satisfactory decorations are obtained, scrape the icing with a spatula, refill the bag, and begin decorating the cake.

Reminders

Consistency — Use icing of a medium consistency for pictures and borders and a thinner consistency for writing.

Angle — Hold the decorator bag at a 90-degree angle when filling in the patterns and accents. Hold at a 45-degree angle for borders and written messages.

Pressure — The amount of pressure applied to the bag will determine the size and uniformity of the decorations.

Extra icing — Keep it covered with plastic wrap or a damp cloth to prevent it from drying out. Rewhip icing frequently to make it easier to handle.

WE HOPE YOU'VE ENJOYED THIS BOOK.
OTHER FAVORITE EARLY CHILDHOOD PUBLICATIONS FROM HUMANICS LIMITED INCLUDE:

— INFANT & TODDLER —

___ HL 038-3	Infant and Toddler Handbook	$12.95
___ HL 049-9	Humanics National Infant-Toddler Assessment Handbook	$16.95
___ HL 085-5	Toddlers Learn by Doing: Activities for Toddlers & Activity Log for Parents and Teachers	$12.95

— ACTIVITY BOOKS —

___ HL 003-0	Child's Play	$14.95
___ HL 014-6	Metric Magic	$ 9.95
___ HL 033-2	Children Around the World	$14.95
___ HL 037-5	Exploring Feelings	$14.95
___ HL 051-0	Art Projects for Young Children	$14.95
___ HL 052-9	Aerospace Projects for Young Children	$12.95
___ HL 058-8	Handbook Of Learning Activities	$14.95
___ HL 059-6	Vanilla Manila Folder Games	$14.95
___ HL 060-X	Back to Basics in Reading Made Fun	$14.95
___ HL 061-8	Month By Month Activity Guide	$14.95
___ HL 066-9	Early Childhood Activities	$16.95
___ HL 069-3	Energy	$ 9.95
___ HL 075-8	Birthdays: A Celebration	$12.95
___ HL 076-6	Scissor Sorcery: Cutting Activities For Early Childhood Programs	$16.95
___ HL 083-9	Fingerplays & Rhymes For Always and Sometimes	$12.95

— EARLY CHILDHOOD EDUCATION —

___ HL 001-4	Looking At Children	$14.95
___ HL 004-9	Alternative Approaches to Educating Young Children	$ 7.95
___ HL 005-7	The Whole Teacher	$14.95
___ HL 015-4	Young Children's Behavior	$ 8.95
___ HL 024-3	Competencies	$12.95
___ HL 034-0	Planning Outdoor Play	$12.95
___ HL 062-6	Feelings	$ 8.95
___ HL 063-4	Nuts & Bolts	$ 8.95
___ HL 065-0	Learning Environments For Children	$12.95
___ HL 045-6	Leaves Are Falling In Rainbows	$14.95
___ HL 047-2	Bloomin' Bulletin Boards	$12.95
___ HL 046-4	Freedom to Grow	$12.95
___ HL 043-X	Storybook Classrooms	$14.95
___ HL 078-2	Can Piaget Cook?	$12.95

— CHILD ASSESSMENT —

___ HL 028-6	The Lollipop Test	$19.95
___ HL 030-8	Childrens Adaptive Behavior Report (CABR)	$ .75
___ HL 039-9	Humanics National Orientation To Preschool Assessment	$14.95
___ HL 054-5	Childrens Adaptive Behavior Scale (CABS)	$19.95

— SPECIAL EDUCATION —

___ HL 000-6	New Approaches to Success in the Classroom	$12.95
___ HL 012-X	LATON: The Parent Book	$14.95
___ HL 067-7	EARLI Program Vol. I	$14.95
___ HL 074-X	EARLI Program Vol. II	$14.95

— SCHOOL COUNSELING —

___ HL 013-8	I Live Here Too	$ 8.95
___ HL 016-2	When I Grow Up Vol. I	$14.95
___ HL 017-0	When I Grow Up Vol. II	$14.95
___ HL 018-9	H.E.L.P. for the Adolescent	$ 7.95
___ HL 025-1	Real Talk Student's Manual	$12.95
___ HL 026-X	Real Talk Teacher's Manual	$ 7.95
___ HL 027-8	Humanics Limited System for Record Keeping	$12.95

— PARENT INVOLVEMENT —

___ HL 032-4	Best Chance Diet	$ 8.95
___ HL 002-2	Working Together	$14.95
___ HL 009-X	Better Meetings	$ 9.95
___ HL 011-1	Dialog for Parents	$ 2.00
___ HL 035-9	Kids Who Hate School	$12.95
___ HL 036-7	Handbook of Reading Activities	$12.95
___ HL 050-2	Parents and Teachers	$12.95
___ HL 053-7	Building Successful Parent-Teacher Partnerships	$ 9.95
___ HL 056-1	Family Enrichment Trainer's Manual	$12.95
___ HL 057-X	Family Enrichment Trainee's Manual	$ 2.95
___ HL 068-5	Love Notes	$19.95
___ HL 070-7	Reading Roots	$10.95
___ HL 072-3	Emotionally Yours	$ 6.95
___ HL 048-0	The Love Book for Couples	$12.95
___ HL 044-8	Parents & Beginning Reading	$14.95
___ HL 077-4	Lives of Families	$12.95
___ HL 084-7	Handbook for Involving Parents In Education	$14.95

‡ ‡ ‡ ‡ ‡ ‡ ‡ ‡ ‡ ‡ ‡ ‡ ‡ ‡ ‡ ‡ ‡ ‡

AVAILABLE FROM
YOUR LOCAL SCHOOL SUPPLIER.
— OR —
CALL COLLECT (404) 874-2176
TO PLACE YOUR ORDER.

Visa/Mastercard Welcome!

HUMANICS LTD./P.O. BOX 7447/ATLANTA, GA 30309

(All prices subject to change without notice.)